D1488328

GUILTY

until proven innocent

The nightmarish, true story of a pastor
falsely charged with the
sexual molestation of children

By Rev. Keith Barnhart
with Lila Wold Shelburne

Introduction by Robert W. ten Bensel, MD, MPH

HANNIBAL BOOKS
Hannibal, Missouri—"America's Home Town"

(Use coupon in back to order extra copies of this and other helpful books from Hannibal Books.)

Table of Contents

Table of Contents

Why We Are Publishing This Book

James C. Hefley, Ph.D.
Publisher

I can think of no more abhorrent crime than for a minister, child care worker, parent, or any adult to sexually abuse a trusting little child for a moment of perverted satisfaction. Especially a minister.

When the media began reporting allegations made by parents in the sensationalized McMartin case in suburban Los Angeles, I was almost sure Peggy Mc-Martin Buckey and her son Raymond Buckey must be guilty. I—as I suspect did most other Americans—wanted them to be convicted. Somehow I failed to notice that the parent who made the initial charges—disseminated by local police and setting off a wave of hysteria among other parents—was diagnosed a paranoid schizophrenic and died the following year of alcohol related liver disease.

When the story of Keith Barnhart's arrest for sexual child abuse first broke in the St. Louis media I was just as certain of his guilt. Everything I saw on TV and read in the newspapers pointed in that direction. It appeared that he had all but been caught in the act. Had anyone asked me then if we would be publishing a book by Barnhart, I would have said, "no way" and stamped my foot in disgust at the thought.

I began having second thoughts after reading an editorial by a church editor friend, Dr. Bob Terry. Bob wrote about political pressure on the prosecutor created by a ratings-hungry TV station to arrest, charge, and convict Barnhart. ". . . A faithful pastor, his ministry, and his good church have been smeared," said Dr. Terry after the trial.

Could this be true?

Had a tunnel-visioned police force, a politically-minded prosecution, a biased and unscientific medical abuse unit in a respected Catholic hospital, an aggressive TV station and other media—had these "professionals" unwittingly committed a misguided, but terrible injustice by presuming Pastor Barnhart guilty of child sexual abuse even before a serious investigation began?

I made some discreet inquiries among people I trusted in the St. Louis area and got the same judgment: Barnhart had been presumed guilty before he was found innocent—an assumption I had made myself. My St. Louis friends said Barnhart was innocent.

After the trial I met with Barnhart and his wife, Lynne, a registered nurse. I decided that their story deserved a hearing and recommended publication of the book you have in your hands.

It happened that the McMartin trial—the longest trial in U.S. history—ended just before writer Lila Shelburne delivered the Barnhart manuscript to us. After 33 months, $15 million, 124 witnesses, and 60,000 pages of transcripts, about all the opposing sides in the California trial appeared to agree on was that the police and prosecutors had made serious errors in investigating, preparing, and presenting their case. The defendants who had spent years in jail, even though they had not been convicted, were acquitted on 52 child molestation charges.

A second sensational trial is due to begin as this book is coming off the press. Ray Buckey faces 13 charges that were unresolved in the first case. It would be presumptive for me to make any judgment on this case or any others in the court process, except to quote editorial reaction in two influential American newspapers to the ending of the McMartin trial:

USA Today, January 18, 1990: "Courts must protect the innocent. That means protection for the children, but protection for defendants as well."

St. Louis Post Dispatch, January 21, 1990: "Child sexual abuse is a horrific crime; being wrongly accused of child molestation is a horrific nightmare."

Reverend Keith Barnhart's "horrific nightmare" is faithfully reconstructed from the recent public records of the police investigation, depositions, subpoenaed documents and videotapes, and the actual trial record of his case. Barnhart's account, along with the probing introduction by Dr. Robert W. ten Benzel, should be must reading for every minister, health professional and therapist, teacher, child care worker, and parent who is concerned about children and justice.

That is why we have published this book.

THANK YOU

To my lovely wife, Lynne for always being there.

To Cave Springs Baptist Church, for caring and standing with me and letting me be their pastor, even while I was accused and prosecuted for allegations of sexual child abuse.

To Lea Haney, for being my faithful and dedicated "Attack Secretary," and to both Lea and Joyce Miller for transcribing the many depositions of the children.

To attorneys Charles E. Bridges and William M. Seiber Jr. and staff for presenting excellent legal defense.

To Jim and Laura Rogers for providing valuable resource material and for making their home an oasis.

To Harold Hendrick, Gary Robnett, and hundreds of other pastors and friends for supporting and praying for me.

To Lila Shelburne, my talented co-writer, whose persistence and attention to detail made this book possible—and to her husband Clayton for his loyalty and understanding during the many months the book was in process.

DISCLAIMER

All names of members of the prosecuting families and my cell mates have been changed to protect their privacy and identity.

All names of the Child Care workers and the church members with the exception of my secretary, Lea Haney, and Bob and Virginia Hull, have likewise been changed.

Dialogue and statements relating to my case are taken verbatim from public records of my initial interrogation at the police station, the depositions, subpeonaed videotapes and transcripts, the preliminary hearing, and the trial proceedings. The dialogue and statements have not been edited for content or grammar, except that in a few instances we have used ellipis marks to reduce redundancy and bracketed words to establish greater clarity.

Any error by myself or the co-writer in presenting and interpreting events of my traumatic experience is purely unintentional and totally without malice.

INTRODUCTION

Child Sexual Abuse:
Where Are We Heading?

by Robert W. ten Bensel, M.D., M.P.H.
Professor of Public Health and Pediatrics,
University of Minnesota

**"If we know where we have been, we would
know better where we are heading."
Abraham Lincoln**

Our society's current issue of sexual molestation of
children began only in 1978 when the National Center for the Treatment and Prevention of Child Abuse
and Neglect included sexual abuse of children as part
of the federal definition of child abuse. This change
in law was subsequently adopted by all 50 states to
require mandated reporting of sexual abuse of
children under age 18 to police for criminal control
and to child protective services in order to help protect
children and help families.

Society responded by reporting more cases of
sexual abuse. We were shocked by estimates that up
to 25-35 percent of girls and 20 percent of boys under
age 18 were being sexually abused. Studies began
documenting the emotional harm done to children
and the professionals in psychology and medicine
were called in to produce techniques which would
obtain better data in interviewing children and medical evidence for confirming allegations. Criminal
prosecution became the major policy to control child
sexual abuse.

Jordan, Minnesota (1984); Cleveland, England (1987); and the McMartin case in Los Angeles (1984-1990) were highly publicized by the media. Now the dust is settling and taken-for-granted concepts and psycho-medical data have been questioned as to their scientific reliability and validity. In other words, are we measuring what we say we are and is the data reproducible?

The presumption of innocence which protects the constitutional rights of the accused was lost in Jordan, Minnesota, but is now being reconsidered by cases before the U.S. Supreme Court (1990) which will determine whether children can testify by closed-circuit TV and allow a pediatrician to testify what a three-year-old told him to the court.

Psychologists and physicians have re-evaluated their professional roles in these cases as to whether they are therapists and healers. The psychologist, physician, and other professionals are not extensions of the criminal justice system, but must "promote human dignity," "be objective," and have their testimony "stand unedited for either side" of the adversarial process. Melton and Limber stress the avoidance of "intruding into the province of such legitimate decison making authorities as judges and juries."[1]

Physicians have now completed scientific studies which "re-emphasize the caution medical examiners must exercise in rendering an opinion as to the significance of medical findings."[2] Dr. Krugman of the Kempe Center states in an editorial that a "hymenal diameter greater than four millimeters alone, reflex anal dilation alone, or a scar at six o'clock is not

---

1   *American Psychology,* September 1989
2   McCann et al, *Child Abuse and Neglect* 13(2): 179-193, 1989.

diagnostic of sexual abuse. As we continue to learn from research findings, we will continue to know more, not less. We may, however, be asked to do less with what we know in court."[3]

The professionals who deal with child maltreatment must be true to their ethics of "human dignity" to "do no harm" and to be as "objective and truthful" as possible. Over the Ark of the Covenant are the words "truth, justice, and peace"—only if there is truth will there be justice and justice leads to peace in the community.

The McMartin case and the many cases like Reverend Keith Barnhart's are testimony of a system gone awry. As a juror in the McMartin case is quoted in response to public outrage: "They did not listen to two and a half years of testimony. I am sorry if the world is not happy, but it was me there, and I can live with it." This reflects the courage and honesty that is needed by all of us who are concerned about children, families, and a just system of intervention which we must use in moderation. If we make mistakes we must learn from them and make appropriate corrections for the present as well as for future generations.

---

3   *Child Abuse and Neglect* 13(2): 106, 1989.

Chapter One

Shocking Allegations

"I've never even had a child in my office."

Morning services were over at Cave Springs Baptist Church in the western St. Louis suburb of St. Charles when the phone rang in my office. The caller identified himself as Sam Walker and requested an appointment.

"What is the matter you wish to discuss?" I asked.

"It involves our son, Chad, and something that happened to him in the Child Care."

I wondered why he was calling me, the pastor. The Child Care was operated by a church board and two co-directors. I had no direct involvement, yet I could hardly turn a parent away who wanted to see me.

"Mr. Walker, I'm unaware of any problem, but if tomorrow evening is convenient, let's make an appointment. In the meantime, I'll talk to one of the Child Care directors and find out what's been happening."

He seemed satisfied.

Later that afternoon I phoned co-director Dora Fenton and told her about Sam Walker's call.

She seemed surprised. "Mr. Walker wants to see you? I thought we had everything all settled about little Chad."

My curiosity was aroused. "What kind of problem did you have?"

"Brother Keith, it wasn't that big a deal. Chad—he's one of our four year olds—claimed one of the two-year-old boys rubbed his bottom with a bar of soap and caused a rash. The Walkers called the Division of Family Services. The DFS came out and investigated and found we use only liquid soap. I thought that would be the end of it."

I called Mr. Walker back and explained that "since the incident has been cleared, I don't see how I can be of any further help."

I put down the phone and pushed aside a faint feeling of unease. I thought little more of it until Dora came up to my office on Wednesday morning.

"Brother Keith, the Walkers have been here today, but they didn't discuss the soap incident. Instead, they were asking if you ever brought children upstairs to your office. I didn't like the insinuation of their question."

The idea of something happening between me and the children was incredulous. "That's impossible," I muttered. "I've never even had a child in my office."

The 1986 Child Care Christmas program was scheduled at the church for the next evening. I rushed into our house just in time for dinner. "Sorry, I'm late, Dear," I called to my wife, Lynne, as Jackson, our golden retriever, came bounding at me, almost knocking me into the lighted Christmas tree.

Lynne greeted me with a kiss. I had told her about the Walkers the day before. "Any more problems at the Child Care?" she asked. Concern lined her forehead as the tree lights reflected in her dark brown eyes.

"Yes, Dora has more upset parents," I sighed. I dropped my top coat over the end of the couch and loosened my tie. "I can't imagine why anyone would ever suspect of me of taking children to my office."

"Well, it sure makes the red flags wave in my mind. But let's forget all of that for now. I'll call the children." Lynne headed for the basement stairway. "Emily, Matthew, Dad's home. Let's eat. We don't have much time, if we're going to get to the program on time."

Lynne turned back to me. "This is the first Child Care Christmas program we've had when I don't have to work at the hospital, and I don't intend to be late."

Our two kids bounded up the stairs. They were hungry. Nine-year-old Matthew's dark eyes and willowy build marked him as his mother's son. Everyone said that Emily, his 11-year-old sister, fair-skinned and studious, took more after me. They were making good grades in a local Christian school where I served on the Board of Fathers. They knew nothing of the problems at the Child Care.

After supper Lynne shooed the kids into their rooms to finish getting ready. I was in our bedroom changing clothes and didn't hear the phone ring. Lynne had just said hello to Dora.

"Lynne, I need to talk to Brother Keith. We've got more problems at the Child Care."

The door bell rang. "Hang on a minute, Dora," Lynne said. "Keith will be right here. Someone's out front."

Lynne opened the door and was shocked to find two county police officers and a town detective from St. Charles staring at her. "Is Reverend Keith Barnhart in?" one of the county men asked politely.

Matthew and Emily had come up behind Lynne. They saw who the visitors were and faded timidly into the background.

Lynne's sense of control gained from her years of work as a registered nurse came into play. She knew she didn't need to let the police in. She closed the door, leaving them on the doorstep and hurried to get me. Then she ran back to Dora waiting on the phone.

"Dora, we've got police at the door asking for Keith. Do you know of a good attorney?"

"Police? Yes, Charlie Bridges. My husband taught him in Sunday School. I'll get his number."

The police impatiently punched the bell repeatedly before I got to the door. "Yes, I'm Keith Barnhart. What can I do for you?"

"Reverend, we have some questions we'd like to ask you down at the police station."

I blinked, thinking that this couldn't be real, but saying, "O.K., I'll get my coat."

Lynne was still on the phone with Dora. Just as I walked out the door, she slipped a scrap of paper into my hand and said something about an attorney's phone number. I carelessly shoved the paper into my pocket, thinking, Why do I need legal advice? I haven't done anything wrong.

Still in an unbelieving frame of mind, I stepped into the patrol car. I wasn't afraid. Why should I be? Since early childhood, I had believed that police were here to protect the innocent. I felt confident that by truthfully answering a few questions, I could clear up any misunderstanding.

It took only a few minutes to drive to the station. The detective directed me through the lobby and into a cold interrogation room: four naked walls interrupted only by a huge mirror framed into one wall—a one way window, I suspected. It was not until several weeks later that I found the mirror concealed a video camera which had taped my interrogation.

A dark scruffy table with two straight chairs provided the
only furniture. The detective pointed to one chair. "Sit there,
Reverend. Somebody will be with you in a few minutes."

I took the chair and found myself looking at my reflection
in the mirror: a 40-year old seminary-educated, bespectacled
pastor of a suburban Baptist church wearing a very traditional brown tweed jacket and matching tie. What could such
a man be doing in a police station?

As I sat there looking into the tall mirror, a line from a
Christmas carol echoed in my mind: "Love and joy come to
you." I didn't feel any love and joy or peace, only a chilling
sense of being stranded. I knew the room must have been
purposefully left this way. The absence of color and decor was
intended to subtly strip the accused of all emotional support.

A tall slender man wearing a light colored trim suit
entered the room. He extended his hand. "Detective Pope,"
he said perfunctorily. Then he read to me my rights.

"You do not have to make a statement or answer any
question; you have the right to remain silent. Do you understand?" I nodded and he scribbled his initials on the paper.

"Anything you say can and will be used against you in a
court of law. Do you understand?" At my nod, he initialed
again.

"You have a right to talk to a lawyer for advice before we
ask you any questions and to have the lawyer present with
you during questioning. Do you understand?"

The detective read several other questions before complet-
ing the ritual. He then read a waiver and instructed me to
sign.

"Do I sign this before I know what is going on here?"

"All I can explain to you is that we are doing an investigation in conjunction with the Division of Family Services.
O.K.?"

"Should I go ahead and sign it?" I persisted, still wondering
why all the formality was necessary for just a few questions.
Detective Pope indicated I should, so I did, then he started
questioning.

"Mr. Barnhart, like I said, we are conducting an investigation along with the D[ivision of]F[amily] S[ervices]. Are you
aware that DFS [is] talking with people where you work?"

"I know they have looked into one situation."

"Could you tell me what that situation was with regards
to?" Pope sat facing me, our knees barely three inches apart.

"... From what I understand indirectly from [Mrs. Dora Fenton] the parents said that one of the boys rubbed a bar of soap on another boy's bottom and caused a rash. The Division of Family Services came out and checked. We don't even have bar soap in the bathrooms. [DFS] looked the situation over and found nothing to substantiate any of the allegations."

"Do you have teachers there besides Mrs. Fenton?"

"There are five teachers in the morning, a couple of cooks, and ... some other workers that come in the afternoon." I named some of them.

After more general questions about the Center's daily hours, Detective Pope asked about my pastoral position at the church and involvement in the school operations. He wanted to know if there had been any other incidents involving the DFS and if there had ever been a problem with the ladies in any of their child care experiences. Then he asked about the church layout and the school's facilities.

"[The Child Care] is in the basement. . . . Upstairs is basically the auditorium with offices and the lower level is an open area with classrooms and fellowship hall, and a kitchen."

"Your office is upstairs?"

"Right."

"With the—you said the auditorium. I guess that's where you hold services also?"

"Right."

The discussion to this point was slow and low key, except that the constant motion of Detective Pope's hands were distracting. I sat back casually in my chair with my hands tucked in my pant pockets.

"So essentially . . . the kids are downstairs with the cooks and the teachers. And you're upstairs"—he waved a hand—"in your office with . . . whoever would come and visit you. Correct?"

"Yeah. There's a secretary there in the morning. I'm usually there just in the morning. . . . I'm hardly ever there in the afternoon."

"You're hardly ever there in the afternoon?" I answered by shaking my head. "Have you ever gone down and visited with the children downstairs?"

"Not in the afternoon, I haven't."

"Not in the afternoon," Pope echoed.

I decided to give him my daily schedule: "I take my kids to

school, [arrive at the church] about 8:30. Go down and get a
cup of coffee. Come back up. Maybe a couple of times a week
have lunch downstairs. "I don't sit with the kids. . . . Then at
12:30 or quarter to one, I'm usually gone from the church.
I'm at the hospital or visiting members."

"Have you ever visited any of the children during the nap
times?"

"No, I have not."

"Not ever?"

"No."

"O.K. Has there ever been any kind of people, you know,
parents of children, come up to you making any kind of
complaints about the care at the Child Care?"

I told him what Dora had related to me about the Walkers'
complaint, that I was bringing children upstairs one at a
time, or bringing a child during naptime. I looked straight at
the detective. "I've never visited with the children at naptime."

"You've never been around the children during naptime?"
I shook my head, wondering how much more redundant this
could get.

"O.K., have you ever—did they ever accuse you of any other
wrongdoing other than just bringing them upstairs?"

"Not that I'm aware of."

"Not that you're aware of?"

"There may have been implications there but Dora, the
director, did not indicate."

"The director did not indicate this. The director is, you said,
Dora?"

"[Co-director] Dora Fenton."

"Dora Fenton. Now, ah, the reason—" Pope seemed to be
searching for the right words. "Another reason why we are
here is we're trying to find out if there's any basis for these
accusations. And if there [is], we want to . . . find out if there
is a possible solution . . . to get the situation resolved." Pope's
voice remained steady, not threatening.

"I can appreciate that. I'd be glad to get the accusations
put to rest 'cause there's no basis for them."

"There's no basis for these accusations whatsoever?" Pope
repeated. Again I just shook my head. It was like talking to
a parrot. "If I were to interview any of these children, there
would be no basis for any of these accusations?"

"None whatsoever."

"O.K."

"Better yet, you need to interview the teachers. The teachers are down there [with the children]." I explained that the same teachers were not scheduled every afternoon, and although I sometimes dropped off kitchen and paper supplies in the afternoon, I didn't go anywhere near the children.

"And you don't even work there in the afternoon?" Detective Pope asked again. I just shook my head.

"Very rarely, if you do?"

"Very rarely, if I'm there."

"Is there any reason why any of these children would make up any of these stories?"

"I have no idea why they would."

"I've been told by a couple of the children that there are incidents you'd be coming downstairs during nap time."

"I'm not down there during naptime," I repeated, controlling the impatience I felt.

"I also had a child indicate to me that there has been some physical contact between you and him."

Now he was starting to get to the point. I wanted to be certain we were both talking the same language. "What would be physical contact?"

"Physical contact would be—uh, I know this is a very delicate situation. Especially between two professional people such as ourselves. But, uh—" Pope squirmed in his chair. "You know—the physical contact that has been implicated is the touching of one's penis."

"No," I answered, irritated by the very thought. I shook my head and answered in slow measured words. "What can I say other than I haven't done it. I have never touched one of the children in the genital area. Never."

"Have you ever taken them upstairs?"

"No, I have never taken any of the children upstairs."

"Have you ever had any urges for this?"

"No, sir!" This was getting repulsive.

Still Pope continued. "I understand some of these urges are sometimes almost uncontrollable for some people. And if there is a situation like this at the school, we want to try to get whatever help we can."

"No, sir. You can talk to any one of the teachers. I'm not around there during naptime. It's just a fact. I am not around there during naptime," I emphasized again.

"But what I can't figure out is why two children specifically would tell me—"

"I can't figure it out either," I interrupted. I sat powerless, hands in my pockets, observing a drama that was being acted out, with me in the lead role. Perhaps it was a good thing that I didn't know that I was being secretly videotaped.

Pope continued. " . . . This was going on, you know. These children are at the age they don't know what is right and . . . . what is wrong. They just do what the adults tell them to do."

"That could be what—you just hit the nail on the head. What the parents have told them to say."

"So you think the parents may have a child. . . ." He mumbled something that sounded like abuse.

"I don't know about that. I don't want to make any accusations. I don't want to get into their game, but I have not taken any child upstairs by himself. I have not touched any child in the genital area—you know, I don't know where they may have got it from."

"Have you ever photographed a little boy?" Pope asked the question casually, the same way he might ask if I wanted a coke.

"No!" I responded, shaking my head. "You could go there right now if you want. It would be right in the middle of the Day Care program, but there's no camera. No camera at the church. I have a couple [of] cameras at home, but they don't even hardly work.

"You know accusations like this," I continued, "you see them on the news and, ah, it's hard, it's hard to defend yourself against, but I have no reason to lie. Because like I said, I am almost hardly ever there. I mean it's very rare that I'm there in the afternoon. The teachers, every one of them, could tell that I'm just not around. I do not come down there during naptime. I'm not around during naptime. I do not take one out during naptime or any other time. I have never had a child upstairs in my office alone or anywhere upstairs." I shifted my glasses again, thinking, I'm beginning to sound like a parrot myself.

Pope pushed on. "You know, I've been in police work for ten years now. I've never found a four year old that would lie to me about a serious accusation such as this. And I—"

I didn't like the corner Pope was trying to back me into so I interrupted again. "Then what you're saying is that you believe the four year olds over me."

"No, sir. No, sir," Pope assured, shaking his head. "I am not saying that at all. I'm saying I've never had a four year old lie to me before . . . . over serious accusations such as this. First of all, they don't know what they're talking about most of the time when it comes to this kind of activity that we're discussing. Understand what I'm saying? So I have to try to find out what's really going on here."

"I can appreciate that."

Pope kept gesturing with his hands. "You know, I don't want to say this side over this side. I'm trying to find out exactly what's going on, and try to remedy the situation before it gets out of hand."

"I can appreciate that very much."

"And, uh, I just—you know, I'm not trying to say that I believe the kids over you, but that it's just hard for me to disbelieve them at their age bracket."

Pope leaned forward in a posture of intimacy, his elbows on his knees and hands folded. "Now if they were eight or nine years old and they were more into the world of telling fibs and telling lies, then I could say, 'Yeah, they may have cooked this together.' But when you're three, four, five, or six, kids all saying the same thing, it's not a situation that is not all that unbelievable. Especially . . . with all the situations hitting the newspapers and TV in say, just the past six months. There's a lot of people in this world that, uh, . . . it's very understandable that a person would have some of these strange ideas and maybe fulfill a couple of their little fantasies or whatever."

"I have no fantasies like that." Emotionally I reeled from the detective's insinuations.

"None whatsoever?"

"No, sir." My answer was flat, void of the emotion I felt churning inside. It had never been my nature to become defensive or lash back in retaliation.

"I guess it is just very difficult for me to say right off the bat that the kids are lying and it's hard for me to say you're lying. I'm trying to find out. I'm trying to get the balance in this. It's very difficult in a situation like this to find out the balance. Where's the line to be drawn? If you could help me?"

"I don't know what else to tell you. . . . Talk to anyone of the staff members to see if there is any basis. Have they ever seen me take a child upstairs . . . ? Ever seen me do anything like this? There is always somebody there. There [are] always two teachers there. There is no way I could take a child out without somebody being aware of it."

"Would they attempt to stop you if you were taking a child out? Or would they just sit back or what?"

His persistent, redundant questions galled me. "I don't know. I've never done it." I feigned a calmness I didn't feel.

"You don't know what their reactions would be?"

"No."

"I hope you can appreciate what I have to go through." Pope was whining, appealing for pity.

"Oh, yeah, . . . I hope you can appreciate where I'm trying to— I don't know at what point to say, 'O.K., when do I need legal counsel?' I am trying to be as open as I can. . . . I've said everything I know to say. I don't know what else to say, so I repeat, I do not take any of the children upstairs. I never touched a child in the genital area. I never met with a child alone by himself upstairs. I just haven't done it."

"And you've never taken a photograph of a child's penis."

"I've never taken a photograph of any child—of any part of their body."

"But I have a child who's saying that."

"And I'm saying I haven't. I never have. I've never taken any photographs."

"So essentially what we have here—we got one person saying one thing and another person saying another. Who am I supposed to believe? That's a question I'm putting to you. Who am I supposed to believe?"

His question didn't really deserve an answer, but I couldn't be silent. "You know, it looks like to me you are going to need to check further for other corroborating witnesses or evidence, to see if there is any. I have nothing to fear."

I leaned forward, and took my hands out of my pocket to reiterate my point. "You know that's what I'm saying, 'I have nothing to fear.' You talk with any of the staff people and to see if there's any corroborating evidence, that at any time I have been with a child alone. I have not. I have nothing to fear there."

"I can appreciate that." Pope got up from his chair. "Would you excuse me for just one minute, please?"

"Will I be much longer, sir?"

"No, not very much longer."

I sat alone in front of the mirror, trying to comprehend the most confounding situation I had ever faced. I knew my innocence as certainly as I knew my name. There had to be some missing factor, some horrible misunderstanding. But by whom? What had triggered this? And did Detective Pope believe me?

I slammed my fist into my hand in frustration. Then I bowed my head and silently pleaded, "Lord, what's happening to me? How can I convince this policeman that I haven't done anything?"

Chapter Two

Intensive Interrogation

"But if it didn't happen, what do I do?"

After I left with the police, Lynne quickly got back on the phone with Dora. Confused and afraid, Emily and Matthew had slipped off to their rooms.

"What's going on, Dora?" Lynne asked with a tremor in her voice. "The police just took Keith."

"Oh, dear God, help us," Dora groaned. "The workers just called from the Child Care. The problems have gone further than the Walkers. Jackie Brady came to get her son, Todd. She went to another mother and said, 'If you know what's good for your son, you'll get him out of here.' Then she pointed her finger at Kathy Haynes [one of the workers] and screamed, 'I'm going to kill you!' That's why I called to talk to Brother Keith."

"But Dora, Keith hasn't done anything. What do the police want with him? There must be some terrible misunderstanding."

"Well, I sure don't know, but I'm heading over to the Child Care. The Christmas program will be starting in a few minutes. You might better stay home and wait 'til you hear from Brother Keith."

Lynne was not one to go to pieces. Nursing had taught her to think clearly in crisis situations. She knew what to do in case of an emergency. Wiping her eyes, she reached for the church directory and dialed the number of Ben Dole, the chairman of the church deacons. The tears came back as she waited.

Ben wasn't home. Lynne called Clyde Jones, chairman of the Child Care Committee, and Bob Hull, pastor of our mission church. "I think Keith's been arrested," she told them. "Please go to the St. Charles Police Station so he isn't alone."

A few minutes later the door bell startled Lynne. "I thought you might like some company for awhile." Bob Hull's wife, Virginia, smiled warmly as she assured Lynne, "Bob's already at the police station, and he'll stay there until he finds out something." The two women sat together in the silent glow of the Christmas tree lights which seemed only to color the evening in somber tones.

Downstairs, at the church, the Child Care workers stood around frightened, wringing their hands. "What are we going to do?" they kept asking each other. By now the auditorium upstairs was filling with children and parents who had come for the program. Ida Smith, our other co-director, a petite grandmother, answered in her sweet strong-hearted voice, "Well, we're going upstairs and we're going to have that program. And we're going to smile if it kills us."

"Yes," Dora agreed, "We can't stand around like cats hanging on to the ceiling." And in her natural take charge way Dora began, "Ida, you're going to have the opening prayer because Brother Keith won't be here. And . . . . "

The workers mingled briefly with the parents and settled the children in their places near the front. When Ida stepped on the platform, she saw Ted and Jackie Brady and their son, Todd, walk in. A quick glance around the auditorium told her the other workers had seen the Bradys too.

"Let's pray," Ida said with only a slight quiver in her voice. And while she prayed the workers wondered, Why has Jackie Brady come back with her son after she accused us of harming him? Is he going to participate in the program? Will she cause another scene?

While the program went on as scheduled, I remained at the police station. After Detective Pope left, I sat alone for several minutes puzzled and bewildered over what was happening. Finally I pulled from my vest pocket the scrap of paper Lynne had given me and read the scribbled name and number. I put it back in my pocket, thinking, Why do I need an attorney? This can't last much longer.

Footfalls clicked in the corridor. "Detective Harvey," the new man announced. Heavier and about four inches shorter than Pope, he provided an interesting contrast with the first detective who had questioned me. Harvey's dark, slightly disheveled hair and moustache blended with his dark shirt making him fit his role of the heavy. "Do they call you Pastor, Father, or Reverend?"

"Brother Keith, usually."

"O.K. Brother Keith is the term they use for you mostly."

"Yes."

After these polite questions, he got right to the distorted point. His speech was confusing and rambling. "O.K., what would—why would two people that are completely—you know, they go to the same school; but for two four year olds to make up a story is really—for one to make up a story is really kind of ironic. But for two of them to make up a story that kind of coincide with each other, unless they got together and collaborated which four year olds can't do. You know that and I know that and so if you've got two four year olds coming in and giving a story—now, I've been doing this for 14 years. . . ." Detective Harvey rambled on about his experience, repeating the popular opinion that young children don't lie about things they don't know about and salting his opinion with examples. "Four year olds may be extremely fearful, extremely scared of something, but they don't lie, O.K? And in my experience, in this particular area a four year old could not make up some of the stories I've heard today. It's absolutely impossible. That's why I asked you what they called you. O.K? Because they call you Brother Keith."

"Right."

"O.K? They said, not the janitor, not pastor—they called you Brother Keith."

"All of the kids do. They know my title."

"That's right. Well, they know you. So it's not like a guy coming off the street and did whatever. It's not like there's any other males out there, not like John, the janitor. It's Brother Keith did this to me, sir. O.K?

"We've got three kids right now—all right? Again, I'm not here to judge. I'm here to explain things to you and gather the truth. O.K? I mean—I'm 40 years old and you what?"

"Forty."

"Forty years old. We know—I'm a man and you're a man and we're going to talk to each other man to man. O.K? You mind if I call you Keith?"

"No. That's O.K." I was becoming a bit impatient with his patronizing talk.

"Keith, I'm not going to lie to you. I have no reason to lie to you. Because I'm here to talk to you one on one. You know—I'm not going to jump, huff, scream, rant and rave. . . ." But he did rant and rave. Finally he said, "We've got one four year old, Keith, that has nightmares and you know what he says when he wakes up from his nightmare? 'I've got to put my clothes on and go back downstairs.' O.K? You know why he says that? O.K?"

"I have no idea," I replied, beginning to realize he would be satisfied with nothing less than a confession.

"Because he's relating that to an incident that occurred upstairs in the Day Care Center. Now this is a four year old having nightmares. This is not something the parents say. One of the other kids saw you the other day when you were getting gas. You know what this four-year-old kid's statement was? 'There's the bad man with glasses,' and he tucked his head down in the seat of the car.

"This is not a four year old playing games, Keith. This is a four year old telling what he knows because this is what happened to [him]." Harvey rambled on. Then in an effort to be diplomatic he said, "And again, I'm not here to judge, Keith. I'm not here to judge you. But I'm here to talk to you. And I'll tell you another truth, O.K?"

"No, you're telling what you've heard today," I corrected.

"Yes, I'm telling you what I've heard. O.K? That's how [we] do our job. If somebody doesn't come tell me something, I've got nobody to talk to. That's why I'm talking to you. I mean it wasn't like the kid come in and said, 'Somebody did something to me.' And then we say, 'My God, we're going to have to try to find out who the somebody is.' The kid tells us who the somebody is. They say, 'Brother Keith.' All right?"

Detective Harvey pushed his chair closer, shoving his face almost into mine. I wondered what could possibly have started such accusations. I didn't yet know which kids were accusing me. How could I explain something so bizarre as these stories? What could I say to make myself believable?

"The kids tells us who the somebody is. They say, 'Brother Keith.' Alright? It's not like we just randomly picked out a name because these kids decided to come down and tell that they had been, you know, confused, touched, whatever you want to say. They tell us who did it. So what are we supposed to do? We've got to pick up Brother Keith, and we've got to talk to Brother Keith."

Harvey elaborated more along these lines, spitting his

words machine gun fashion, obviously aiming to disarm and intimidate.

"Who has it in for you—the parents?"

"It has suddenly developed very quickly." I explained about the Walkers, the allegations, and the DFS investigation.

Harvey interrupted. "Keith, let me tell you something. . . ."

"Let me finish this," I insisted. "[The Division of Family Services] could find nothing to substantiate the allegation. I called the family back. I said, 'I've talked with my [Child Care] director. I can see no benefit meeting with you. I have nothing further to add.' Then the next thing I know, yesterday morning the couple is in the church . . . with the director, making accusations that I had taken the children upstairs. I have not. How do you defend yourself against such accusations?"

"O.K. Let me ask you something. Let me tell you something. We've got victims. Four-year-old victims."

"That makes me extremely sad."

"I know. I understand. It makes me extremely sad because I've got a brand new baby and I've got two other kids. O.K? Like I said, I'm not going to jump up and down, rant and rave. I don't do things that way. You've got your job and I've got mine. O.K?

"We've got two four-year-old kids. We've got a third one who is a little bit hesitant to talk to us because he is scared to death. O.K? If something like this happened—O.K. Let's go hypothetical. If something like this happened and you did do it, O.K., I'm not asking you to make an admission, just hear me out. Hypothetically, if something like this happened and you say, 'I didn't do it. Prove it,' then I have to do my job. And my job is to work a case and to prove something. And how I'll do that is take these little four year olds and walk them into court in front of 12 people in a jury. O.K? And I'd say probably eight out of twelve in the jury probably have kids the same age. And I'll have these two four year olds, and I'll have the third one standing by, and I'll have them get on the stand and I'll ask them their story. And they're going to tell their story and then you're going to have to get up and say it didn't happen. O.K? That's one way of looking at it. That's one way of doing it and I don't want to do it that way.

"For God's sake, and you're a Christian man, for God's sake, if this happened, you don't want to take it in front of a judge. You don't want these little four year olds coming up and saying, 'Brother Keith did this.'"

"But what if it didn't happen, what do I do?" I asked, expecting logical advice. His answer stunned me.

"Keith," he said, jutting his face even closer to mine. "I'm going to tell you the honest truth, I think it happened."

Detective Harvey continued with his hypothetical scenario trying to confuse and frighten me. I desperately wished for a reasonable explanation to clear up this dreadful misconception. I had none.

"We've got two four year olds who—God forbid, I hate to have to drag them into court and have them get up on the stand and say, 'He did it. Brother Keith did it.' And one of them is going to be scared to death because he's scared to death of you. He has nightmares over you." Harvey continued to elaborate about the children, claiming he'd even tried to trick them.

"So what's really the kicker is that outside your domain and outside their school, they see you getting gas. And this little four year old, you know, was petrified. Because in his own mind all he could do was put everything in that school because that's where all of this happened. But he sees you outside the school and he just goes frantic. And he says, 'There's the bad man.' You know what that woman did? She came to church that following Sunday after seeing that bad man. And she didn't know who you were. She copied down your license number—she copied down your license number after her little boy had his head buried in the seat. They ran the license number and it comes back to your car. She says, 'I can't believe this man would be the pastor of the church.' She goes to church and sees you up there Sunday morning. And lo and behold, she walks in and she says, 'That's the bad man.' O.K? And this woman has got to come back home and try to convince her boy that this church is not bad, the Day Care Center is not bad, and you're not bad. Knowing in her own mind she would just as soon grab you around the throat and drag you around the room. O.K?"

I sat shaking my head. "Why you have one [child], much less three, I have no explanation." I felt helpless and numb with shock.

Harvey shrugged. ". . . Could be a problem that we've got some parents who are all upset with Brother Keith. You have no reason to believe that anybody would do this to you?"

"I'm afraid not," I answered, knowing if there were some

motive, some reason for all this it would make more sense.

The interrogator began firing another string of questions. "Do they know where your office is [located]...? Would there be any reason why—for one of the boys to tell me ... that you locked the door after he got in there?"

Still not getting the results he wanted, Detective Harvey got personal. "How old are your kids, Keith?"

"Nine and eleven."

"Would you believe it if your four year old came and told you something like this...? You would believe him, wouldn't you?"

Harvey was circling his prey, shooting arrows to wound and confuse, yet the only pain and confusion I felt came from wondering where such scandalous accusations could have originated and why?

"Keith, I believe these four year olds."

"And I'm telling you that there is no basis in fact for what they have told you," I answered in a controlled but desperate voice.

"Well, you see, that's where we have the problem, Keith. O.K?" Harvey elaborated still more.

"Well, I—"

"I believe them so much," Harvey interrupted, "that I'm trying to give you every opportunity—"

"I understand that—"

"For you to talk to me. You know what. . . ."

I was getting aggravated, really aggravated at his continued insinuations. "If there was anything I could say to you, I would say it, but the only fact is I HAVE NOT DONE IT!" I spoke slowly with my hands open before me. Harvey kept trying to interrupt me but I just kept talking. "I don't know where this has come from. I WISH God would TELL me where this came from. I have not done it."

"But you know what's gonna happen, Keith? Your [Child Care] kids are going to say you did it. Then we're gonna go to—we're going to put them through all kinds of misery, all kinds of hell. . . ." He was again implying that I would force him to traumatize innocent children in court.

"What would you do," I interrupted, "if three kids came up and said, 'He was out and he did this. . .?' How would you defend yourself? If these same accusations came against you?"

"I would know. O.K?"

"I would know, too. And I have not done it. . . . You know, we might as well finish our discussion. You know, there is nothing more I can say to you. 'Cause I did not do it."

"Then you're probably going to have to pay the consequences for it."

"For being accused of doing something I didn't do?'"

"Yes, sir."

"I didn't do it." Because I had so much honor and respect for the police, it was still hard for me to realize they had already decided I was guilty. The painful drilling continued.

"How am I going to tell three four year olds they are liars. . . ?"

"I'm not saying that."

"I know that. But how am I going to tell these four year olds it didn't happen?" Again Detective Harvey repeated the allegations. ". . . Now if you want to get up and explain that to all or half of St. Charles, that's entirely up to you."

"I didn't do it." I emphasized each word and felt them bouncing back—unheard, deflected by some unseen barrier.

"What I'm saying though—if you say, 'Detective Harvey, . . . prove it,' then that is what I'm going to have to do. Then that's what I'm going to do," he repeated.

"I don't want to tell you to go out and prove it. That's not my point."

"I understand that."

"I'm just simply saying I cannot imagine or explain whatsoever where the stories came from. I have not done it and I don't know what else to tell you. Now, I hear . . . very definitely what you're saying. If there was anything I could tell you for an explanation, I'd be more than glad to tell you. I can understand your position, but I have not done it. I have not touched any of the little children, . . . taken any pictures, pulled their pants down, been with them alone."

Harvey was obviously unconvinced. ". . . I want to lay something out to you. O.K? With what we have, we'd be willing to take [you] to court. O.K? I think your biggest concern would be to show us and prove to us this didn't happen. I mean—you know, wouldn't you want to convince us that this didn't happen?"

"I would if there was any way I possibly could."

"O.K., have you ever heard of a polygraph? Lie detector test?"

"Yes."

"Would you be willing to take a lie detector test? . . . You've got to convince these little four year olds, their parents, and now the police department, because this is part of the system. O.K?"

"Is this polygraph admissible evidence in a court?"

"No."

"What benefit would it be to me?"

"You convince me."

"Convince you?" I'd been trying all night to convince this man of my innocence.

"That's right. It would be a step in the right direction for you to take the polygraph. . . . Only because I've done this before and I have not had a four year old lie to me yet. Not on something like this, you know. . . .

"Your main concern would be that you want to do everything you possibly can to cooperate with us. Right? That's why you came down here. That's what you want to do. . . . If I set up a polygraph tomorrow, would you take one?"

I was suspicious. "I'd probably have to think about it overnight. . . . Perhaps seek legal counsel and see what's involved. You know, I've never had one before." If the polygraph was so valuable, why didn't detectives save themselves the strain of interrogations? I wondered. Why weren't the results admissible in court and why did I need to take the polygraph before he decided to check out the parents?

At this point Harvey left the room briefly with the promise he wouldn't keep me much longer. I glanced at my watch. It was 8:45. The Child Care program would be over.

I would learn later that both Mr. and Mrs. Brady and their son, Todd, stayed for the program, and Todd even participated. From the platform Todd could plainly see the door of my office. Yet there he stood smiling and singing, showing no fear at all, the workers told me later.

Ida was there talking to the Bradys when some policemen came in to get Kathy and bring her down to the station. Kathy, with her natural trusting innocence, had turned to Dora and asked, "Will you go with me? I'm scared."

But I knew none of this when Detective Harvey entered the room again. "Keith, one of the accusations we have is that a photograph—we don't know if a photograph was taken or not. A camera was produced and a little boy says, '. . .Brother Keith took a picture of my penis.' O.K? . . . Do you own any cameras?"

"Yes, I do."

"O.K. Do you ever take your camera to the church with you?"

"No, I never bring them to church."

"You never had—had a camera in church?"

"Not during Child Care time. Maybe during some special event but I—it probably hasn't been there within the last year since the Child Care. . . ."

"O.K., Keith," Detective Harvey interrupted, "I want to tell you something. Um, with the information we have right now—you know what a search warrant is?"

"Yes, sir."

"We have enough information to get a search warrant and go to church and go to your home. And I know you wouldn't want us to go to your home with your wife there. . . ."

The room had become stuffy. I was tired of the psychological games, the pressure tactics, the intimidation, the senseless repetition. But Harvey kept on.

". . . Can you imagine how devastating it would be if we went to your house with a search warrant . . . ? We don't want to do that. I want you to take a polygraph. In fact, if I could set one up tonight I'd like you to take one tonight. But I couldn't do it. I'd like to have you take one tomorrow, though."

I waited a moment to answer. "I have no problem. I have no concern about telling the truth. I'm just not positive that polygraphs are all that accurate."

"O.K. I've used them in a lot of cases. I'm one hundred percent sure that if you're telling me the truth, I'll know it after the polygraph. I have no doubt. . . ."

I was restless. When Harvey finally left the room again, I stretched, wrung my hands to release the tension, then leaned forward. With an elbow on one knee, I propped my chin in one hand and flicked a piece of lint off my pants with the other. I had leaned back in my chair again when Detective Pope returned.

"Mr. Barnhart, I've talked to Detective Harvey and he's indicated to me that you're not too hip on the idea of a polygraph examination." Pope continued trying to convince me, parroting that if I passed the lie detector test, he too would be on my side. This whole interrogation was becoming more redundent all the time. I decided Pope and Harvey deserved a plaque I had at home:

DEPARTMENT OF REDUNDANCY DEPARTMENT.

"But it's not admissible in court," I challenged. "It's not admissible anywhere as evidence. So it is only—"

"It's strictly to help me come to a decision," Pope broke in, "as to who I should believe. Who should I believe, four year olds or a 40-year-old man? Now, we know the newspapers have been loaded with people who have abused children, molested children, whatever you want to call it. They've had two or three soccer coaches [in the St. Louis area during] the past two years involved in illegal and immoral activities with young children. O.K? I'm not here to judge. If that's what they want to do, that's fine as far as I'm concerned, just don't mess with my kid. That's the way I look at it."

Detective Pope went back to the polygraph but my mind strayed. What did he mean by "if that's what they want to do, that's fine...?" He couldn't be serious, or could he? I really didn't know. I'd become oblivious to everything but the penetrating shock and seriousness of the accusations. Revulsion, anger, impatience all raged through my mind draining me of energy. ". . . I've got these kids telling me, boom, 'Brother Keith did it to me . . . pulled my pants down . . . took a picture of my penis.' What [is the jury] going to believe?"

All I could think was, "DEPARTMENT OF REDUNDANCY DEPARTMENT."

I looked straight at Pope. "If I convince you, then what happens?"

"If you convince me, there's no problem. . . . But right now we have three four-year-old kids, little bitty kids, who are going to come up to the judge and say, 'Judge, this is the man who did it.' . . .

"And the jury is going to sit there and say, 'Well, we heard about this before in the newspapers, we've seen this on TV, and we've read about it a lot . . . in *Time. . . Newsweek. . . .* They're going to say, 'God, here in town!' Ministers do it, priests do it, rabbis, soccer coaches, everybody. No one's exempt. . . . There's even been a cop or two accused of this stuff, too, that have done it. O.K? It's not a situation that is strictly for the poorer people and the less educated people, it's not that kind of situation. Some of the brightest minds in the world have had tendencies toward children. Socrates. Aristotle. You know, the great Greek writers of long ago."

Pope rattled on. When would he ever run dry? I glanced at my watch and realized they had been going at me for nearly two hours. Finally I agreed to the polygraph test which Detective Pope said he would arrange for the next morning.

"Thank you very much," he said and turned to open the door for me to leave.

As I walked through the lobby, I heard someone say, "Reverend, you have some friends waiting outside."

There were Bob Hull and Clyde Jones, the two church officers Lynne had called, sitting and waiting for me in Bob's car. The cold air did little to revive my numbed senses but their familiar smiles produced warm relief. I got in the car and briefly related my situation. I couldn't tell if I made any sense or if their silence was the same shock I felt. After a minute or two, Clyde got out to get in his car and drive home. Bob drove me to my house, saying little on the way. Lynne's anxiety escaped in a rush of words as Bob and I walked through the door. "Keith, I'm so glad you're home. They didn't arrest you!"

"Not yet," Bob answered. "It may be sooner than you think, but not yet. They were pretty serious down there."

Virginia Hull, who had remained with Lynne, stepped quietly over to Bob. Concern showed in her round gentle face.

"Keith, is that true?" Lynne asked in disbelief. "I thought you'd get things straightened out."

"I thought so too," I answered, almost falling into my recliner. "I think Bob's 'not yet' is a pretty realistic comment." I didn't know what else to say. I felt as if there had been a death in the family. It all seemed so unreal, so impossible, so unbelievable.

"It's probably not as serious as it seems tonight," Bob said. "Anybody that knows you, Keith, knows there's nothing to it. The police will talk to the Child Care workers tomorrow and it will all blow over and go away. We all know you didn't do anything. Let's pray, though, before we leave."

After Bob and Virginia left, I filled Lynne in on more of the details. "They went on and on for about two hours telling me they believe I have sexually molested some boys. What could I say? If I haven't done anything, I haven't done anything. It looks as if I'll have to prove I'm innocent."

Lynne sat speechless for a minute, fear and horror and shock all evident in her face. Then with her hands turned up helplessly, and desperation shrinking her voice almost to a whisper, she uttered, "But Keith, this is America, where everyone is innocent until proven guilty."

We sat for a moment frozen in immobility. It was our dog Jackson's gaping yawn that pulled us back into life. I went for his nightly dog bone as Lynne repeated the nagging question, "Where did such accusations come from? Keith, there's no way, there's no basis for any of this." Her reassurance was soothing.

"I am tentatively scheduled to take a polygraph test tomorrow, but I need to talk to an attorney first. I think you gave me a name before I left."

"That number's for Charles Bridges. Dora Fenton says he grew up in their church and he's really good."

I went to the phone and called him.

"You don't want to take a polygraph test," Mr. Bridges advised. "I'll call and cancel it for you in the morning."

I made an appointment with the attorney for three the next afternoon and then called Dora. "Hi, I just wanted to check and see how the Child Care program went."

"Like a night I wish I could forget." Dora related the incident with Jackie Brady threatening Kathy, and the police taking her away afterward. "The police had her in tears, Brother Keith, when she came out of the interrogation room. She was frightened to death."

"Why did they question Kathy? I mean, why Kathy?"

"Well, I guess it's because they know she's there a lot in the afternoons. From the way Kathy talked, it seems to me they think you and Kathy have conspired together." Dora talked fast and didn't stop until she asked, "What all did the police ask you?"

"The gist of it,—well, they seemed to think I've molested some of the boys."

"With the open door policy and the way we rotate the workers? Brother Keith, that's impossible. You're never around the kids."

After I said goodnight to Dora, the voice of Detective Harvey kept swirling through my mind: "I believe these four year olds, Keith. . . . I think it happened."

Finally I got into bed where Lynne and I followed our usual custom of praying together. When we finished, I felt comforted for the first time that evening.

Chapter Three

Threatened by Parents

"I have never touched your son."

I awoke early Friday wondering what the new day might bring. The events of the night before were like a dream, far away and unreal. Everything seemed the same as I went through my morning routine. Water still ran from the shower head, my tooth brush hung in the same place. Jackson stood wagging to be put out, and Sheba, our blue point Siamese cat, wound herself between my feet begging for breakfast. I could hear Lynne in the kitchen setting out breakfast dishes and making lunches for the children.

After we ate I dropped Emily and Matthew by Living Word Christian School on my way to church. Shortly after I arrived Charlie Bridges called. "I've talked to the police and canceled your polygraph appointment," he reported. "They will probably come out to look around. You don't want to give them permission. They may even decide to search your house. If they have a search warrant they can search anytime, whether you're home or not."

It wasn't long before the police were standing inside the church foyer. "No, you may not search the church," I answered in response to their request.

"We can go get a search warrant," one officer responded.

"You'll have to do what you have to do," I replied. "My attorney advised me not to give you permission and because I'm paying him for his advice, I'd better take it." Still I was puzzled.

I didn't understand myself why I couldn't cooperate with the police investigation. They were looking for truth and I had nothing to hide. I wanted to cooperate with the investigation in any way I could.

After receiving more information from Dora, Lynne and I

went that afternoon to the attorney's office. We had only a
brief wait in the small unpretentious outer office before Mr.
Bridges introduced himself and led us to his office. "Just call
me Charlie," he said in his somber voice. From then on he
was Charlie while we remained Reverend and Mrs. Barnhart
to him.

I liked him immediately. He was my height, about five foot
eight inches, but smaller framed, and his fair complexion
contrasted sharply with his thick brown natural curls. He
motioned for us to sit down in the two chairs facing his desk.
Through the wall of windows to our right I admired the view
of the Missouri River slowly slipping by just three blocks
away.

He picked up his yellow legal pad and leaned back in his
black executive office chair. "Reverend, when did you first
become aware of a problem?"

I began filling him in with details of events of the previous
Sunday. Sam Walker's call for an appointment. The Walkers
complaint that a little two-year-old boy had rubbed a bar of
soap on Chad Walker's bottom while the boys were in the
bathroom.

"How old is Chad Walker?" Charlie asked without looking
up from his yellow pad.

"Four."

"Must be an awfully tough two year old." Only a sparkle of
amusement flickered in our attorney's eyes as he lifted his
head and asked, "What happened next?"

"Walkers reported the soap incident to the Division of
Family Services and the DFS came to the church and investigated. They cleared us because we don't have bar soap. We
use liquid soap.

"Dora told me the Walkers had withdrawn Chad on
November 19, over two weeks before Mr. Walker called me.
Since my information was second hand and because neither
the Division of Family Services nor Dora Fenton felt any-
thing had happened, I called Mr. Walker back and told him
I didn't see how I could be of any help to him.

"He wanted to know about punishment for children. I told
him that the teachers have them sit in a chair apart from the
other children or stand in a corner. Then he wanted to know
the name of the DFS investigator and I gave that to him and
told him again that they had cleared us."

Charlie didn't look up from his note pad so I kept on

talking, telling him about Dora coming upstairs to my office the following Wednesday to tell me that the Walkers had unexpectedly showed up. "They didn't seem to want to talk about the bathroom incident," she said. "Instead they asked if I ever took children upstairs."

"Anybody that knows Keith, knows he isn't the kind of man to spend time playing with children," Lynne noted. "They asked if he ever took the children upstairs one at a time during naptime, but Charlie, he's never there in the afternoon. The Child Care workers will all vouch for that."

"Did anything else occur before the police came to your house?"

"Yes, Thursday morning Dora came to my office again saying there were at least three families concerned about their boys." She'd been on the phone all morning trying to find out something specific but even the complaining parents Dora knows quite well wouldn't say anything."

"Have the Walkers called again?" Charlie asked.

"Not us, they haven't. But Dora told me they've called the Bradys and Farrows. I understand they're all good friends. Dora said one of them called another parent, a Mrs. Manard, and because she works nights she called her husband Thursday morning and told him kids were being molested and he wasn't to bring their children in. He did anyway and told one of the workers he didn't believe a word of it, that this was a good Child Care."

"So Mr. Manard doesn't believe the others but we still have three families upset?" Charlie Bridges clarified. I nodded. He asked several more questions, filling a number of pages with notes. When he looked up I wondered if he believed my innocence.

"Can you elaborate more on your opinion about the polygraph?" I asked.

Charlie laid his legal note pad on his uncluttered desk, leaned forward in his chair, and stated, "I've talked to the prosecutor's office and from what I've heard the police have already made up their minds; they believe you are guilty." Charlie's mannerisms were slow and deliberate, and his voice soothing as he continued his explanation.

"When I worked in the prosecutor's office we would sometimes have a suspect take the polygraph twice, each time from a different expert and we'd get opposite results. So, number one, I don't have faith in the polygraph. Number two, if the polygraph examiner believes at the time that a person's guilty, there's no way the examiner is going to say the suspect passed the polygraph. I've never seen a police polygraph examiner say a person passed when the examiner thought the suspect guilty. At most, he'd say it was inconclusive.

"For example, I knew of a child abuse case where the accused took a lie detector test and passed it. But then the police came back and said it was administered wrong. They wouldn't accept it even though it was administered by their own people. It's a catch 22, Reverend.

"The key thing to remember is that a polygraph is still not admissable in court." Charlie leaned back in his chair and said in a grave tone that left no room for questioning, "If you flunk the polygraph the police tell the parents and then the media."

I understood what Charlie was saying but I kept thinking that as soon as the police investigation got underway and they talked to the Child Care workers, the allegations would be dropped.

"You understand, of course," Charlie warned, "that if this does get into the media it's going to be devastating." Lynne and I both tensed at hearing this.

"There is no way to tell now but it sounds like that is where things are headed."

We left Charlie Bridges' office that Friday afternoon sobered and quiet. Lynne voiced her fear as soon as we reached the privacy of our van. "Keith, how will we ever face people again if this hits the news. I just don't think I could handle that." Shaking her head in bewilderment she continued, "It just doesn't seem like God would let that happen."

I pulled out of the parking slot. "I'd like to think none of this is happening but we both know that God doesn't promise anywhere in the Bible that bad things won't happen to us." I checked my rear view mirror before turning into the traffic. "Anyway, I really doubt much more will come of it."

"I wish I could be so confident," Lynne sighed. "I couldn't believe you two. You and Charlie Bridges sat there talking as calmly as if you were discussing the weather. I bet you two could talk a fly to sleep."

"Well now, maybe so, I've never tried that before," I quipped, fully aware that my undemonstrative temperament sometimes irritated her.

The next evening at the supper table we tried to prepare

our kids for some of the things that could happen. "It's possible something could reach the news and we must remember that if people don't know all of the facts, things can be said that aren't the truth," I carefully explained.

Lynne passed around a plate of Christmas cookies. "Kids, one thing Mr. Bridges mentioned was that the police may decide to search our home."

"Will they take our toys and mess up our things?" Emily wondered.

"Honey," Lynne answered patiently, "They'll just look around, they're not interested in your things." Both Emily and Matthew looked relieved.

"We just want you to understand that we may go to the library or shopping and come back and find our house searched," I continued. "They don't have to put anything back so we may have to make our beds and put our belongings back in drawers. We have nothing to hide so we have nothing to fear. Your mother and I just want you to be prepared."

Before finishing supper, I thought of my parents who lived in DeSoto, Missouri, about 50 miles south of St. Charles. "Lynne, I think I'll call them. I hate to make something big out of this, on the other hand, if it does hit the news, I want them to hear it from me first."

Dad responded in his typical stoic way. Mom's voice had a worried edge to it when she said, "Let us know what happens, Son."

I then called Bob, my only sibling, who owns a Radio Shack store two hours away in Salem, Illinois. I could sense my older brother's embarrassment when I mentioned the specific sexual acts the police had confronted me with. Our conversation was awkward. Sexual matters had never been talked about in our home and as adults, we still felt uncomfortable discussing them. I promised to keep him informed. Lynne called her brother and sister and they told her parents. Mrs. Blackman kept saying, "Not Keith, this can't be happening to Keith. That's just so foolish."

We'd been concerned for Lynne's father for some time because he had been having occasional spells of anger and forgetfulness. Sometimes he'd just act confused so we were surprised by his clear minded response when he asked, "Do you have money for legal fees?"

Lynne thanked her father for the inquiry and said, "Well, at this point, Daddy, we're not expecting any charges to be filed."

Up to this time, only the Child Care Center workers and major church officers knew what had been happening. We felt it necessary to inform our church family at the next Sunday morning service.

After concluding my sermon I announced, "Clyde Jones, the chairman of our Child Care committee has a special statement to make." I stepped down from the pulpit and sat beside Lynne.

Clyde set his notes on the pulpit and nervously cleared his throat. "During the last few days a very serious matter has come to our attention." A tense quietness filled the sanctuary as Clyde related the recent events. "Suspicions have passed from one parent to another and now the parents of at least three boys have jointly alleged child abuse and Brother Keith is the focus of the investigation."

Lynne reached over and took my hand as the congregation sat stunned. It was the first time I'd heard my name mentioned publicly in connection with the alleged abuse. I was thankful that Clyde had judiciously omitted the term "sexual" when he mentioned child abuse. Still I felt my face flush and I dropped my head. "But I haven't done anything," I told myself. "I have done nothing to be ashamed of and I will not allow myself to act as though I have." Taking a deep breath I forced my head up and listened intently as Clyde continued.

"Anyone who knows Keith recognizes the absurdity of the allegations, but there is an investigation and it is a very serious matter." Clyde drew out the last three words for emphasis.

"Let me be quick to say that the safety and welfare of our children always has and always will be our primary consideration. I don't fault the parents for their concern for their children, but I know if they knew Brother Keith, they wouldn't be doing what they're doing." Heads nodded in agreement throughout the congregation.

"Nor do I fault the police for their investigation into the matter. I assure you, however, I believe in Brother Keith. The Child Care staff and the committee stand behind him."

Clyde cleared his throat and shifted his weight. His grey hair and quiet demeanor added gravity to what he said next. "Due to the serious nature of the allegations Brother Keith has retained legal counsel and one of the major things counsel has advised is that we are not to discuss this matter with anyone. We are told this is a necessary precaution for Brother Keith's protection.

"The Bible tells us to speak not evil of one another." Clyde expanded briefly on this thought and closed by encouraging all to pray "for Brother Keith and his family, but let's not stop there. We need to pray for the children, their parents, the police investigation, and the Child Care workers."

Fellow church members swarmed around us after the service ended. People shook our hands, hugged us, and some cried. "We're standing behind you all the way," came from every direction. And, "Whatever it is they're accusing you of, Brother Keith, we know you didn't do it."

I stepped into my office to answer the phone. "This is Channel Five, St. Louis. Reverend Barnhart, may we interview you regarding an accusation of child abuse occurring at your Child Care?"

I pulled in a deep breath and hesitated before speaking. "I have no statement to make," I replied, still hoping to clear the misunderstanding without media involvement. I was surprised that they had already heard about the accusations.

That afternoon, as I tried to rest at home, my apprehension increased. "There's nothing to any of this," I kept telling myself. "It will be cleared up soon."

A good supportive crowd turned out for the evening service. We were just breaking up, when someone announced, "Channel Five's van is parked outside on the street." The news hit me like a blast of cold winter air. Lynne and I exchanged worried glances.

Two men from the church approached the TV van, providing a distraction for us to get in our van. When we arrived home we programmed the VCR to record Channel Five's evening news. For a moment my heart stopped beating when I heard the anchor man promise an "exclusive report."

"Parents in St. Charles tonight think their children may have been abused at a child care center. Good evening, I'm Dick Ford. . . . Tonight John Pertzborn learned of the incident and talked with some of the parents. . . ."

The camera panned the living room of a private home decorated for Christmas. Stockings hung on the fireplace and several somber faced couples sat visiting together. I recognized none of them. A new voice continued the narrative.

"Since last week these parents all pulled their four-year-old children out of this school. The parents say they have been noting changes in their children's behavior. The St. Charles police are investigating, the parents say. This weekend the parents all got together and compared stories and discovered their children's stories all match." I sat and stared at the TV. This whole thing was just too incredible to be true. I still could hardly believe what was happening.

The camera focused on a bearded man. "They can't be in a room alone. They have to have someone with them all the time." The name James Farrow appeared on the bottom of the screen and his voice cracked with emotion. "Our son, he's very touchy about his clothes and when you touch him—"

A full-faced brunette in a bright red sweater added, "We suspected it—maybe as far back as September, it's when the discipline problems started." Keri Walker was the name at the bottom of her picture.

"They must be the Walkers who asked Dora if I had taken their children upstairs," I said to Lynne, as Mrs. Walker made her appeal.

"If you have children attending or have had children attending we'd like you to talk to the police."

The anchor man ended his "exclusive report" by adding, "No charges have been made. . . . The St. Charles police have made appointments to take the children to Cardinal Glennon Hospital for examination Thursday." Then he repeated Mrs. Walker's appeal for parents to call the police department. A phone number flashed across the screen as I was telling Lynne, "I still can't imagine what started all this."

"At least no one mentioned any of our names on TV," Lynne consoled. "It's bad enough the way it is but that would be unbearable. Keith, I just don't think I could stand up to that."

We rewound the video and watched it again. Lynne asked, "Who are those other parents? I didn't know any of them so later that week we asked Dora to watch the video with us and identify my accusers.

On Friday morning, Dora Fenton, Sam Baker, chairman of the church trustees, and I met with attorneys Mike Shea and Don Kohl and engaged them as counsel for the church and the Child Care. The attorneys advised, "You may talk with and cooperate fully with your church insurance agent, however, do not talk with the police or anyone else." I still couldn't understand why we were not to talk to the police.

Why couldn't we help them by giving honest input into their investigation?

"It sounded like they're certain," Sam said, "that we will be facing either a criminal charge or civil suit. Isn't it interesting in a criminal case they will have to prove guilt beyond a shadow of doubt but a civil suit is determined if preponderance of evidence shows against the Child Care?"

"Yes," I agreed, "and if the scale tips even slightly against me in a civil suit, the jury can rule against me."

I called Charlie Bridges late that afternoon. "I've spoken with the prosecuting attorney's office," he said, "and they talked about issuing one charge but decided against it. The police are taking several boys to the SAM Unit—"

"The what?" I interrupted.

"The Sex Abuse Management Unit at Cardinal Glennon Hospital. They don't plan to make any charges until after the reports are back; that will be next week."

"The medical exam will prove there's nothing wrong with the children." I was sure of that.

I felt even more encouraged when I heard his next comment. "It's hard to say for sure, but I think the allegations may be falling apart."

I told him about our meeting with Shea and Kohl and he agreed with the church and Child Care counsel that we cooperate fully with our insurance agent. "However, don't give a statement to them directly," he warned. "Everything you give them must go directly through me, otherwise the prosecuting attorney can subpoena the information."

It still bothered me that neither the Child Care workers nor I could talk to the detectives. We had nothing to hide. We all knew the allegations were impossible, the very layout of the church made it impossible. I asked Sam Baker, "Could you ask Shea and Kohl if there is anyway the Child Care workers can talk to the police so we can clear this up?"

"Keith, the police are trying to get evidence to build a case against you," Sam explained. "The police get brownie points by clearing their books and bringing charges. To use a very trite cliche, anything you say, can and will be used against you. Now is not the time to talk." It was beginning to dawn on me that the police really were building a case against me, although emotionally, I still found it hard to accept that they were doing a biased investigation.

I scanned the newspapers daily, holding on to the hope that

any misunderstanding would still be cleared up. On Friday,
December 19, a small article appeared on page six in the *St.
Charles Journal*: "The St. Charles Police Department began
an investigation December 11 of the Cave Springs Baptist
Child Care Center. . . . Lt. Patrick McCarrick . . . said the
department had received complaints involving five victims.
. . . The allegations concern one individual. . . ." This was the
first reference in print to the problems. I felt relieved that
the story wasn't on the front page.

We began getting disturbing phone calls late at night. I
called my brother, Bob, at his Radio Shack store in Illinois
and explained our problem. "Do you have an answering
machine we can use for awhile until this blows over?" He
promised to bring one on Christmas day when we were all
going to our parents in DeSoto.

Lynne had to work at the hospital on Christmas evening,
so we had only one day to spend with Mom and Dad. After
dropping Jackson at the kennel, we drove down Christmas
Eve.

Other than answering a few questions Lynne and I avoided
discussing the Child Care problems and enjoyed the family
fellowship and food. During Christmas dinner Bob and I
served Mom's traditional chocolate cake. When Mom noticed
that we took our usual pieces from around the outside edges,
she quipped, "I really ought to serve you boys just a batch of
frosting."

"Yeah, we know, Mom," I teased, "You've been threatening
that for how many years?" Bob stood by licking his fingers.
We all enjoyed a good laugh. We left DeSoto in the early
afternoon, so Lynne could report on time at the hospital. I
hooked Bob's answering machine up after we arrived home
and that night it recorded only a couple of hang ups.

The next day we all hopped in our minivan to pick up
Jackson from the kennel. On the way we stopped at Shop-N-
Save for dog food and a few other groceries. As I backed into
a space next to a grocery cart return, Lynne glanced at me.
"Keith, that woman over there is staring at us. She's the one
that's loading her groceries into that gray pickup and she has
a little girl with her, but she keeps staring. Keith, she looks
like that Jackie Brady we saw on TV." Lynne talked in a tight
low voice so our children behind us couldn't hear.

"What are we waiting for?" Matthew complained. "Let's
go in."

"We need to sit here for just a minute," Lynne instructed, and she started looking through her coupons. I watched as the lady got in her pickup and pulled out in front of us. Then she stopped and leaned on her horn. When we refused to look at her, she finally pulled away.

Lynne wanted to get the dog food and get away. I wanted to go ahead and get the other things we needed. While we were standing in the checkout line Lynne whispered, "Keith, there's a man over there in a sweat suit, he looks like Ted Brady. He's not buying anything—just staring at us." It appeared that Mrs. Brady had gone home and told her husband where we were, and he had come to look us over. We paid for our things and pushed our cart over to the bagging counter, feeling the eyes of Mr. Brady boring into our backs.

"I'll go get the van," Lynne volunteered.

"No, let's just stay together," I said. We quickly finished bagging our groceries, then headed for the van. The kids, who had become aware of the stares, scrambled in. While Lynne and I were putting the groceries in the back, we saw Mr. Brady stomping in our direction across the parking lot. Lynne and I hurried to get in.

"Keith, we forgot the dog food," Lynne cried. "It's still in the bottom of the cart. Start the van," she said, opening her door. "I'll get it." She had so much adrenalin going, she probably could have picked it up with two fingers, but I objected.

"I'll get it. Lynne, you know it's too heavy for you." I was scared and half expected to get punched. As we both stepped out of the van, Brady shook his finger at me and yelled, "You'd better stay away from my son."

"I have never touched your son," I answered in a strong steady voice as I put the dog food in the van and closed the back door.

"How can those ladies at the Child Care trust you?" he screamed. "How can you call yourself a man of God?"

"Keith, please get in the car." Lynne's voice was insistent with fear as she saw Brady getting more and more angry. From having worked with emotionally disturbed patients she knew their violent strength and was afraid Brady might attack me. "Get in the car, please," Lynne urged again. As she shoved the cart into the return, I forced myself to walk calmly around to the driver's door.

"If you think it's going to end here," Brady ranted, "you're wrong."

"You are crazy, just leave us alone!" Lynne pleaded, distracting his attention momentarily from me. "We've got our kids in the car." Her voice was no match for his.

As I climbed into the driver's seat, he continued screaming, his face torrid with rage. "I don't care if your kids are in the car, I'm going to say what I want to say." His chest heaved as he thrust a clenched fist high. "How dare you tell our kids Santa Claus will be angry with them!"

"You know nothing," I shouted as Lynne slammed her door.

"Tell that to the police and counselors!" he screamed. I slammed my door, more from fear than anger. My whole body trembled as I began pulling out of the lot.

In the sudden silence of the van, I heard Emily's thin shaky voice. "I'm scared, Mom." I turned and saw her freckles dominating her ashen white face.

"It's all right now, Emily," Lynne comforted. "No one's hurt." I glanced at Matthew, who sat frozen in silence, his dark brown eyes saucers of fear.

"I just kept thinking," Lynne explained after we got on the highway, "Brady wore a sweat suit and they don't have pockets so he couldn't be hiding a gun or any other weapon."

I reached over and took Lynne's icy hand, amazed at her protective aggressiveness. Something Lynne's mother had once told me about her shyness as a child suddenly flitted through my mind: "When I'd introduce her I'd have to pull her out of my skirts. So I started her in dancing school when she was three. By the time she was in tenth grade she not only had her teaching certificate, she'd overcome her shyness."

On the way home we stopped at the kennel and got Jackson. When we arrived home I saw the message light blinking on the answering machine. Thinking there might be some word from Charlie Bridges, I pushed the play button and waited. A male voice spoke. "All the naked little boys say Merry Christmas." It was disgusting. How much more of this would we have to take.

During the next week, several of the Child Care workers retained their own attorneys. The reality that the police were basically trying to build a case against me kept coming around and each time it hit harder and harder. I jotted a notation in my daily planner. "Make plans in case of arrest, ask Charlie to estimate bond."

Charlie thought the bond would be $100,000 with a 10 percent allowance. "It's very common," he explained, "for a judge to grant the defendant freedom with only 10 percent of the bond posted in cash. Then if the defendant doesn't appear in court, he's liable for the full amount." This was some encouragement, but we prepared for what we believed could be the maximum. Just in case the full $100,000 should be needed, arrangements were made to post three properties for bond, our house, my parents' home, and Bob and Virginia Hull's residence.

On New Year's day I was rewinding the answering machine when the red light came on and the phone rang. A lady asked, "Is this the Reverend Barnhart who abused those little boys?"

"I have done nothing," I replied.

"They have proof that you did."

"Who is this?"

"Someone you don't know," she said and hung up. Already Lynne and I had found it difficult to make ourselves go out in public because we never knew who we might run into. Now it was becoming almost as difficult to answer the telephone or listen to the answering machine.

The harassment, however, didn't stop with annoying telephone calls. One January afternoon I left the church to pick up Emily and Matthew from their school. Cutting through the Timberidge subdivision, I noticed a charcoal gray pickup following a short distance behind. My stomach knotted when I realized it was Jackie Brady. I didn't want her knowing where our children went to school so at the bottom of the hill I turned into the parking lot of an apartment complex where one of our elderly members lived. It was easy to see Mrs. Brady drive by as I walked into the housing area. I knocked on the lady's door and while waiting saw the gray truck roll by again. I knocked again but no one answered. I waited until I knew the truck was gone before going on for the kids.

The incident of being followed made Lynne and me feel more vulnerable. After the children were in bed that night we talked about our uneasiness. "I never know who's going to show up at the door anymore," Lynne worried. "I keep wondering if and when our house might be searched, just hoping they'll do it when we're here. Keith, I don't even like to leave the house anymore."

We both recognized, however, that we had to maintain our daily schedule and face the events of each day as they came. Our prayers together that night were the last words we shared before drifting off. The phone woke us both at 1:25 a.m.

"It won't be long now." The chilling voice sounded like Ted Brady.

Some of the calls were baffling, others unnerving. One man whispered, "Jelly and Cissy were your downfall." A female caller announced, "Hi, this is a child molester and I don't like these machines any more than you do, but I have to use them because I s___ around with kids."

The nasty phone calls weren't limited just to our home. When Lea Haney, my secretary, answered the phone at church the caller would often hang up on her. A few days later a lady called and asked for me. "May I say who's calling?" Lea asked in her soft southern drawl.

"Never mind," the caller said, "I'll just leave a message. Tell him that I just dropped off a tape at the police station of him and a young boy having explicit sex. The police will be in to pick him up in about two-and-a-half hours. Bye-bye."

"Why don't you let me screen all the calls from now on?" Lea suggested. I happily agreed. From then on Lea wouldn't let anybody talk to me without stating their name and reason for calling. For her birthday I bought her a cup that said, "Attack Secretary."

Charlie Bridges called to say, "I've talked to John De-Vouton, one of the assistant prosecuting attorneys. They haven't decided what they're going to do. That's a good sign. Since they haven't issued charges, they most likely haven't gotten what they wanted or needed from the [Sexual Abuse Management Unit at Cardinal Glennon] hospital or they wouldn't be so indecisive."

I told Charlie about the episode with Mr. Brady in the parking lot and being followed by Jackie Brady. "We're getting a lot of harassing phone calls too," I added.

"I'll talk to the prosecutor about this. They should have the police tell the parents to stay away from you. It certainly won't help their case any."

Charlie called again on the morning of January 13. "They still don't have enough evidence. They're taking more children in for counseling. The prosecuting attorney told the police to go back out and do more investigating."

I shared Charlie's latest report with Lynne at lunch. "He also says little Tim Raymond claims he was hit and something stuck up his anus. Tim's stepdad is supposed to be taking him in for counseling."

"Keith, how long can they wait before bringing charges?"

"Well, I asked Charlie about that too. He said the statute of limitations is three years. He thinks they'll probably do something in the next week or two but it can go on a long time."

The next day Dora told me about a conversation she'd had with one of the mothers of a child in Child Care. "The mother said, 'I talked to Detective Miller and he said it looked like they were all false allegations. He asked me if I had taken my child out of the school. When I said, 'no,' he said, 'Good, then it didn't disrupt his life.'"

Other than the unrest of waiting, the next few days were peaceful. The upsetting phone calls stopped for the time being—a direct result, we figured, of Charlie talking to the prosecutor. However, Charlie could do nothing more for us until charges were filed.

With uncertainty of the future hanging over me like a hangman's noose, I read from Isaiah 26, "The steadfast of mind Thou wilt keep in perfect peace, because he trusts in Thee. . . ." I mulled these thoughts over and over much like a cow chewing it's cud. I was leaning very hard on the promises of God these days and He was giving me peace.

I kept going to the office in the mornings as before. On January 22 the Child Care cooks made chili, and because they knew it was one of my favorite meals, they let me know that it was being served. Lea went down to get my lunch. Since the allegations had started, I no longer went downstairs during the Child Care Center hours.

I was on the phone counseling someone when I heard a strange voice in Lea's office. I excused myself to see who it was and found myself face to face with Sue Gaylord, the mother of Tim Raymond. Well, not really face to face, she was much taller than me.

She immediately began telling me how bad I was. "I'd like to find the stick you used on my little Tim," she declared. I tried to maintain my composure as she continued her harangue.

"What makes you think you can take my son on walks?"
she demanded.

I answered as calmly as I could. "I don't know what you're
talking about. I haven't done anything to your son. I've never
touched your son—"

"Oh, sure, sure. If I wasn't a Christian, you'd be dead now."
I didn't know what in the world this woman was going to do
so I just stood there, feeling the cords in my neck jumping,
and trying to appear calm.

Finally she said, "I'm going downstairs and check with the
Child Care workers and tell Dora something." I followed her
to the office door and locked it behind her. Then I went back
to counsel the individual still waiting on the telephone.

Dora came up a little later. "I understand you had a visitor
a while ago." I nodded and smiled thinly.

"Well, she came down and stood over my desk and said, 'I
just came here to make my peace with the pastor, or
whatever it is you call him.' Then she said, 'I'd like to find
the stick.' I couldn't make any sense out of that, so I just let
her rant and rave. She walked around for awhile and finally
left."

After gaining my composure, I called Charlie and told him
about Mrs. Gaylord's visit. "Knowing her husband's an attorney, I don't think he'll be happy when he finds out about her
outburst."

"I doubt that he'll be very happy with her," Charlie con-
curred.

"She was obviously very upset but I think she was just
letting off steam."

"Well, I'll tell the prosecution, they should know about it.
If the prosecutor decides not to press charges then the
frustration of the parents will come to a head."

That evening Channel Five reported from in front of a St.
Charles psychologist's office. ". . . Tonight parents of the
children involved met with a psychologist at this office to talk
about the findings. Meanwhile, [Police Officer] McCarrick
[who had interviewed some of the children] says his case is
suffering because some people refuse to talk at all. . . . They
say they believe one person is involved but charges have not
yet been filed."

The TV reporter went on to say that Cardinal Glennon
Hospital had found evidence of abuse.

Lynne sat across from me dazed and shaking her head. "I

just knew the medical reports would clear you, Keith. And to make matters worse, the police are making it sound like we are refusing to talk because we have something to hide."

Dora called as soon as the news was over. "Brother Keith, I can't argue with medical science, but just because there's some kind of evidence it doesn't mean you've done anything." Dora quickly changed the subject. "Oh, by the way, I found a verse in Psalms 31 and it says, 'Let the lying lips be put to silence.' It just seems to me that if King David could pray that way we can too."

"I don't know why not," I agreed.

On January 28, Dora brought a letter to my office she'd just received from the DFS. I immediately called Charlie and read part of it to him: "Division of Family Services have reason to suspect that these children were not adequately supervised as two stated they had been in the upstairs with Brother Keith and no one else. . . . Cardinal Glennon's SAM Clinic has also found physical evidence of sexual abuse which further corroborates the children's statements."

"Does it say what they are going to do?"

"It does not," I assured him.

I hung up the phone and leaned back in my chair. Charlie still couldn't find anything out from the prosecutor's office about what they intended to do. How could Cardinal Glennon Hospital say there was physical evidence? Why was I the only man being investigated? Nothing about any of this made sense. There appeared to be no motivation or reason for any of these crazy accusations. How could "evidence" be found when we knew nothing had happened? Could a person be found guilty before being proven innocent?

Chapter Four

Closing in on Me

"They were sending the message that I was guilty."

Our life took on the pattern of a never ending roller coaster ride. Continual rumors and bad reports kept threatening to send us into an emotional tailspin but constant prayer and encouragement from friends and sometimes people we didn't even know lifted our spirits and gave us confidence to continue our battle.

Harold Hendrick called. I knew Harold mostly by name and reputation as president of the St. Louis Metro Baptist Ministers Association. Harold was pastor of Parker Road Baptist Church in a northern suburb of St. Louis, and a host on the radio interview program, "Encounter." "Brother Keith, according to the news you've been having quite a problem over there. I just called to encourage you and let you know I'm praying for you." I thanked Harold for his thoughtfulness and gave him a run down on facts Channel Five hadn't addressed. "There is really not a whole lot we can do until the prosecution decides whether or not to file charges," I noted.

"Is there a basis for the allegations?" Harold asked. "Have you ever spanked a child or done anything that could be interpreted as something else?"

"Well, it makes a good story but even that's not true. Other than being pastor of the church I have no involvement with the Child Care."

"Let me know if there is anything we can do," he offered and I knew he was speaking for the ministers association as well as himself. Over the next months I came to expect Harold's reassuring calls regularly.

Andy Mueller, a local business man who had lived most of his life outside of hallowed halls and stained glass windows, dropped by to see me. "For six and a half years I carried a badge and rode the midnight shift as a special deputy with the St. Charles County Sheriff's Department," he said. Andy paused and tapped the ash from his cigarette. "I'm not proud of some of the things I did as a police officer to get confessions. I know how they work."

I'd met Andy about two years earlier and at that time he accepted Jesus Christ into his life. It was then Andy said to me, "Keith, it took me six years to figure out who the Higher Power was I'd been hearing about. A man's life is in fibrillation without Jesus." He had lots of questions about God and the Bible at first and we had lunch together nearly every week.

Andy exploded when I first told him about the allegations. "Shorty, there ain't no way you could have done that." His voice was adamant as we walked across the parking lot. "Keith, you're no cold hearted person. You're like the brother I never had, you're always there for me. I'll tell you my answer before I even ask the question." Andy stopped, dropped a cigarette butt, and rubbed it into the blacktop, then we started walking again. "No matter if you're innocent or guilty, if you tell me you're innocent of these charges, I'm going to give you support like you've never seen before. If you're guilty, if you tell me, 'Ya, I did,' and you want to confide and share it with me one on one, I'm gonna still support you and I'm gonna suggest I go with you to get some help. Now the question is, are you guilty?" We stopped again right there in the parking lot, our eyes locked, and we read each other's souls.

"I didn't do it," I said, not defensively, just as a statement of fact.

"That's good enough for me, Shorty. I knew it," he said as we walked into the restaurant for lunch. "I go over to the church and mow the yard in the afternoons 'cause my schedule's flexible. You ain't never there." Andy lit another cigarette and took a draw, all the while shaking his head. "I remember you calling me in to set up tables one Wednesday night for supper and the kids come around hugging your legs. Those kids ain't afraid of you."

We gave our orders and Andy leaned forward, hands clasped together, both elbows on the table. "I'm gonna tell the prosecutors and the bailiffs who you are. I know most of them from my deputy days. Why I'd leave my two daughters with you before I'd leave them with a baby sitter I might know casually."

I guess no family, much less a church can claim 100 percent agreement on all issues all of the time and our church family was no different. Al Johnson was a bugler blowing his own tune. First of all, he thought we should not seek legal counsel but rely only on the Lord. Neither I nor the other church leaders felt legal assistance implied lack of trust.

"Al," I said, "the Bible teaches there is wisdom in the counsel of many. We simply feel that different individuals have expertise in various fields, including law."

Al also felt we should totally cooperate with the police. I'm sure he felt as I once had, and didn't realize they were actually trying to build a case against me. On February 11, Al visited me at church and told me about a visit he'd had with Charles Gaylord, the stepfather of Tim Raymond, one of the little boys who had made accusations. "Mr. Gaylord presented himself very professionally," Al reported. "He told me there are seven boys making allegations."

I was disturbed that Al would make contact with the accusing families, but not terribly surprised. "Did he say what the kids are accusing me of?" I asked, trying not to let my feelings cause a rift between us.

"Yes, he did. Some of them say you took them for a drive. Others say you took them to your house, and described a bathtub." Al wondered if they hadn't meant the baptistry. "Some described a room with a lot of wires."

"I suppose they could be thinking of the sound system in Lea's office, but I don't know when they might have been in there, except the door is always open when she's there."

"Some described something like a refrigerator," Al continued. "Mr. Gaylord asked if we had one upstairs and I told him no. He also asked if you have a Polaroid camera."

"The police asked me that, Al, and I told them I did but the flash attachment doesn't work and I've never had the camera at church."

Al went on to say the kids were hysterical at times. "Some of the boys claimed you molested them three or four times."

"Do these parents know why the prosecutor hasn't pressed any charges yet?" I asked.

"According to Gaylord, the prosecutor doesn't have the evidence. There's one other thing." The tone of Al voice changed somewhat as he continued. "Gaylord also said his son Tim claims you took him to the room where we have church council meetings and put a stick up his butt." Al's eyes gripped mine. "Keith, he's really convincing. The Gaylords' are very sincere and they believe something really did happen."

"I have no doubt they are sincere."

After Al left, I tried to put myself in the position of the accusing parents. They had been told by medical professionals that their children had evidence consistent with sexual abuse and for some reason they believed I did it. I'm sure they were feeling as frustrated as I. They couldn't find evidence of my guilt and I couldn't convince them of my innocence. I wondered how long this deadlock would last.

Later that evening I talked with Lynne about Al's visit with Gaylord. "I almost get the impression, after talking to Al, that if it came down to believing the children or me, he would go with the children. But he said his wife had seen on Sally Jesse Raphael's program that children can make up stories like this, so I think he's trying to see how these children can do that."

"Well, on that he's not alone," Lynne agreed. "We'd all like to know how innocent children come up with these stories."

We started getting abusive phone calls again. Late one night in early February we recorded a male voice with other people talking in the background. "Whether you escape the law or not, you're going to answer for what you've done, and you know what that means." Was this someone who was just letting off steam or was he really planning to carry out a threat?

On February 12, Charles Gaylord came by the church. "I'm here on a friendly visit, you don't have to respond or answer questions. I just have a few things I'd like to say," he explained.

I hesitated, recalling the threatening confrontation with his wife in my office just days before. However, I reasoned, if I listened to him, maybe we could unravel this appalling misunderstanding. I motioned for Mr. Gaylord to be seated on the dark brown couch just to the left of my desk. He was older than I expected. His demeanor coupled with his silver streaked hair which receded past his ears created an air of dignity. I agreed with Al, Charles Gaylord did come across professionally. He opened the conversation after I sat down.

"First of all, I apologize for my wife coming over and confronting you as she did, even though I can sympathize with her feelings."

"I understand," I replied, nodding my head.

"We know this must be hurting your church, you must want this resolved."

"Yes, we'd like to have it cleared up too."

"I want you to know I don't believe everything a four and a half year old says. What I'm wanting to know, is there any middle ground where we might be able to let the workers talk? It seems like everyone's jumping into holes and not talking."

"I know what you're feeling. We have checked with the church attorneys to see if there was any way the workers could talk to the police with an attorney present. We have nothing to hide. The attorney said, 'Now is not the time to talk.' We hire attorneys to give us legal advice. Mr. Gaylord, you're an attorney, I'm sure you agree it would be foolish not to follow their advice."

"Well, yes," he agreed. "I may talk to Kohl and Shea; they are your church attorneys, correct?"

"Yes, they're the ones to talk to. In fact, some of the Child Care workers are talking to them today." He kind of laughed and I wasn't sure why.

"With the physical evidence and all the allegations, I believe something has happened and I'd like to find out what, so we will know how to help our little Tim. Other parents are feeling the same way." He talked about a meeting the parents had with the police. "Some of the parents fell apart because there's such a high level of frustration."

"There's frustration on our side too," I countered, "but there's nothing we can do without our attorneys' approval." Gaylord seemed to understand and rose to leave. As I returned to my desk from walking him to the door I felt like each step took me deeper into the quicksand of suspicions. Would he describe my office to other parents within the hearing of his son? Could he have misunderstood something I said, misread my silence? I sighed and went back to work on a sermon.

When I went home for lunch I noticed the drapes were drawn. Lynne was upset because she'd noticed a car driving slowly by our house several times. As soon as we started eating I told her, "Peg from the Child Care called this morning. She was on her way home and she saw a blue Mazda pickup driving slowly through our subdivision so she pulled in behind it. "Peg didn't recognize who was driving until Todd Brady stuck his head up and waved. Peg followed Mrs. Brady right past our house."

"But why, Keith? Why are they doing this to us?" Lynne cried, her eyes caverns of both anger and fear.

"Well, Al Johnson said the kids were saying I'd taken them to our house," I answered, trying to maintain the calm I didn't feel. "Maybe the parents are seeing if the boys can identify it."

"From now on," Lynne snapped, "I'm keeping the curtains closed. I don't want to run the risk of somebody looking in. There's no way we can defend ourselves if those kids come halfway close to describing the inside of our house."

Charlie Bridges phoned a couple of days later. "Channel Five called today and they've talked to the police." Charlie's steady voice seldom revealed anything.

"Oh, yeah? What's happening now?"

"The police have finally gotten the written reports back from Cardinal Glennon Hospital with what they say is documented evidence of sexual abuse."

"Oh, no," I groaned.

"I refused to give the station a comment and told them to talk to Shea and Kohl who are representing the church and Child Care."

"Anything else happen?"

"I called DeVouton, the prosecuting attorney assigned to your case, to find out what's going on. He's talked with some families and will talk to the others next week. I guess the families are pushing their state representatives to put pressure on the prosecutor's office to file charges and the prosecutors are getting aggravated. The PA won't be pressured into filing charges."

"Well, there's been a few things happening on this end too." I gave a quick summary of the nasty phone calls, Al's visit with Gaylord, and Gaylord's visit with me. "I think the parents are frustrated, Charlie, because none of the workers can say anything to the police. The parents are sure something has happened, but there's not enough evidence to prosecute. I have a feeling Gaylord was trying the sympathetic approach when he said, 'We know it must be hurting your church, you must want this resolved.'"

"How's your church attendance doing?"

"It's good and people are still joining. I couldn't ask for better support."

Charlie cautioned me again not to talk with any of the families. "They could say you said or did something you didn't and it would only make matters worse. Oh, by the way, I've gotten the word that you've taken some kids for walks in the woods."

"Oh really?" I laughed, no longer shocked by anything. "I wonder when I'm supposed to have time for all of this?"

On February 19, I received a message to call Marianna Riley of the *St. Charles Post*. I was a bit surprised because so far the newspaper had only run the one small article back in December.

"Reverend Barnhart, I'm calling about the civil suit being filed against you by the Gaylords and their son, Tim Raymond. It has to do with the child abuse but the suit is calling it 'battering.' It's for six million dollars."

"I have no comment," I replied, stunned.

"So you want to deny it?" she pushed.

"No comment," I repeated, remembering Charlie's request not to discuss my case with the media."

"May I ask who your attorney is then, I'd like to call him."

"Charlie Bridges represents me." I got on the phone with Charlie immediately after talking with the reporter, "Hey, what's going on?" I asked, expecting an immediate explanation of the civil law suit.

"I touched base with DeVouton today," Charlie began. "He's talked to all the families and one of the boys is opening up and beginning to talk. I don't know which one though. There's some talk now about your being a member of a Satanic cult.

"Satanic cult! Where is all this coming from?" I heard the frustration in my voice. "Charlie, there's got to be some explanation, something we're missing."

"Well, maybe we've got time to find it, Reverend. DeVouton now says it could be a month before they file charges, but it still looks like they are going to file something." Obviously Charlie was not aware of the civil suit.

"I got slapped in the face today with reality, Charlie. A reporter, Marianna Riley, from the *St. Charles Post* just called and said the Gaylords have filed a six million dollar civil suit against me.

Charlie hesitated a moment before he calmly predicted, "The prosecutor's not going to like that very well, it might show their motive to be financial.

"But there are a couple advantages to trying the civil suit before the criminal suit. The Child Care workers can give depositions in which information may persuade the PA not to file a criminal suit. In the civil suit we can have access to police reports before the preliminary hearing. On the other hand it can make your defense more difficult. If we have to defend a civil suit first, we might have to give away our defense for any criminal suit.

"If any reporters call you again, refer them to me. If they ask you directly if you did it, say, 'No, I did not.'"

Lynne and I had learned by now that Channel Five would be the most likely of the three major TV stations to carry any news of the civil suit, so we set the VCR there for the evening news, and after supper we played it back. We were both dismayed as we watched that night.

Reporter Al Naipo sat across from Mr. and Mrs. Gaylord in the living room of their home. "I look out my window every morning," Mrs. Gaylord explained, "and see the church and, and his van parked out there . . . ."

The anchorman picked up the narration. "The person Sue Gaylord is talking about is the church's Reverend Keith Barnhart. On behalf of their son, they're suing Barnhart for six million dollars. . . ." This was the first time my name had been connected publicly to the sexual abuse of the little boys. I felt smothered by the hideous lie and pulled hard for a breath of air. I recalled Hawthorne's Hester Prynne and the pain she bore from her scarlet letter but the searing pain I felt from the media's brand burned even deeper because of my innocence.

Reporter Naipo continued. "Probably the main obstacle of the St. Charles police making their case was the fact that no one here at the school had been cooperating with the investigation. . . ." Lieutenant McCarrick, from the St. Charles Police Department, appeared on the screen. "We feel [the employees of the school] probably have information that would be helpful. On the advice of their attorney they refuse to talk."

"Keith, that's not true!" Lynne's eyes snapped with anger. "Those detectives interrogated both you and Kathy. I can understand them not listening to you since they think you're guilty but Kathy denied everything too."

"Well, not only that, but Ida [the co-director of the Child Care], let them into her house. From what she told me, the police assumed I had done things and kept saying, 'Well, now when this happened,' and Ida would stop them and say, 'Nothing happened.' They wouldn't believe her either."

"And Ida wasn't alone, Keith. Brenda, another Child Care worker was there, remember? She went over to see who was at her mother's house and when she got there the police started questioning her and she kept telling them, 'Nothing happened.'"

We listened closely to Lieutenant McCarrick's statement on the VCR: "This kind of crime alleged here is . . . despicable and if you're not going to get involved in this kind of crime because of your own self interests, then I think you have a problem."

Lynne and I were both exasperated. "Keith, almost every one of the Child Care workers has told me they'd knock the doors of the police station down and talk if they believed what they said would not be twisted and used against you. Those women aren't looking out for their own self interests."

"I agree, Honey, and by accusing the women of not getting involved, McCarrick is making it appear as though we have something to cover up."

The following Sunday I made a statement to my church family. "There are three reasons why I can continue to hold my head high and still try to serve faithfully as pastor of Cave Springs Baptist Church. First of all, all of the allegations which have been made against me are totally false. There is absolutely no basis in fact for any of them.

"The second reason is because of the prayers and support from my family, my church family, and friends. Your expressions of love and confidence—well, I just couldn't keep going without you. You have no idea how much I appreciate it when you tell me you're praying for me.

"The most important reason is the strength and power of the Lord that keeps me and my family going." I was amazed and gratified as I looked into the faces of my congregation and saw the love and confidence portrayed in their smiles.

"We need to remember that these parents are not our enemies," I added. "The Devil is the father of all lies and he is the one we must rebuke. We need to keep our focus on the

Lord Jesus Christ and not on the circumstances or on others."

The next morning, I saw ugly, distorted black obsenities sprayed on the outer wall of our white carport. I called my friend Andy and told him about the sordid message. Andy came right over and repainted the carport.

No comfort zone was left. When we went out we scrutinized faces, fearful of another public attack. Threatening phone calls continued to invade our privacy both at home and church. And now that our home had been defaced, we felt it necessary to take even more precaution. In addition to keeping the drapes closed at all times, Lynne began locking all doors. "We've got to be careful not to leave ourselves vulnerable so they can put something, drugs, pictures, anything into our vehicles with the windows or doors open," Lynne pointed out. I agreed and started locking the van in the carport even when I came home for lunch.

"Where is the balance between taking precaution and overreacting?" I questioned.

"How desperate are our accusers?" Lynne countered. Both questions hung in the air between us, unanswerable.

Charlie called me at my office a few days later. "I think the Gaylords have filed suit out of frustration. They want the workers to talk and this will provide a legal means of forcing them to talk under oath. They'll have to wait 30 days for you to file an answer before the workers can be forced to give depositions."

"Then what happens?"

"We wait. It'll take four to five months after the 30-day period before it's put on the court docket."

It was over lunch that Lynne and I could talk freely and Lynne always asked if anything had happened. I related my latest conversation with Charlie and added, "He's talked to the prosecutor's office and they're not very happy about the law suit either. It puts more pressure on them to file criminal charges. After sharing the latest scraps of news, I mentioned a promise from Psalms that kept coming to my mind: "How precious is Thy loving kindness, O God! And the children of men take refuge in the shadow of Thy wings."

As our circumstances became more precarious both Lynne and I struggled daily with our own personal fears by not allowing ourselves to withdraw from our normal activities and daily routines. "Keith, I hate going to work," Lynne said one afternoon as she was leaving the house. Her expression was pained with a deep groove carved across her normally smiling face. "Everyone watches the news, what will I say?"

"I've noticed you have your name tag off and your ID badge on backwards."

"I just don't want to deal with any of the patients who might say, 'Hey, wait a minute.' If they ask my name, I'll just tell them, 'Lynne.'"

Being recognized as the "molester's wife" wasn't Lynne's only worry. "Keith, what if they arrest you while I'm gone, will they take the kids too? What if you're at a meeting and the police come to search the house, can you imagine how scared the kids will be?"

Even in the midst of Lynne's anxiety, I often saw her drawing strength from her own relationship with God. I wondered how I'd manage if my wife relied completely on me and if our marriage could handle the ongoing stress if one or the other of us continually drained the other emotionally.

We both took comfort knowing that Emily and Matthew never had to face humiliating questions or taunting from their schoolmates. Lynne and I thanked God for their Christian school and caring teachers.

My secretary's daughter was not so fortunate. Lea confided one day, "One of her best friends at school asked how she could stand to have her mother work with that child molester." Several of our church children had to face similar embarrassments in the public schools.

In past years I'd asked myself what would be the worst thing that could ever happen. For me, I'd always felt it would be to go to jail, but I'd never thought I would have to face even the possibility. The thought of prison was far worse than the fear of cancer. I couldn't allow myself to dwell on any of the possible consequences. An involuntary shiver surged through me every time I thought about prison. I had to keep my mind on other things. Lynne felt the same way.

Sometime after the initial shock of the civil suit wore off, Charlie called again. "Sounds like there may be another family involved, Reverend."

"Oh, no." I didn't even try to disguise my sigh. "Did they say who it is?" We still didn't know for sure how many families were involved.

"Apparently someone came forward after the suit hit the news. This boy says you've urinated on him or something." The thought made me want to throw up. I sat numbed in silence, the phone pressed to my ear. A prickly heat crawled up the back of my neck and my face flushed. The tension was really getting to me.

I wasn't the only one, however. Dora came to me in the church office one morning during the first week of March. Her face showed the strain of several months. "Brother Keith, I hate to say this, but we're wondering if it might be better to close the Child Care at the end of this month instead of waiting until June. The stress and anxiety is really taking it's toll on the workers."

I nodded. "Yes, I'm sure it is. It seems inevitable that we're going to have to close. What's the attendance now?"

"We were running 50 and we're down to 20. The workers didn't make much over minimum wage in the first place and now they're getting only half pay, and our income is not meeting our expenses. But the biggest thing is the risk factor, Brother Keith. If you can be accused, we can all be accused."

I couldn't blame them for their concern. Dora and I agreed to call a committee meeting to talk about closing the Child Care.

At the suggestion of Bob Hull I accepted a phone call from a woman I'd never met before. "Hello, I'm Laura Rogers. Welcome to the family of the falsely accused." I wasn't sure I liked being welcomed into such a family but the voice I found myself listening to expressed genuine love and concern. I was intrigued.

For the next several minutes she told me about a couple she called Bob and Judy. After rearing their nephew for ten years the natural mother decided she wanted her son back. Through a chain of unbelievable events that followed child abuse accusations, Bob lost not only his nephew, but also his own two daughters, his home, and his job.

She told me about another victim. "John was rearing his daughter alone until she had an accident at school and was taken to a hospital for stitches in her scalp. Because it was hospital policy, she underwent the routine exam for 'abuse.' The doctor decided her vaginal opening was larger than usual so she was taken from her father and John found himself facing charges of sexual abuse.

"I could tell you of several more tragic incidences," Mrs. Rogers noted, "but I'm mainly wanting you to realize you're not alone in your circumstances." By the time she said, "Tell me your story," I realized I was not the first person to be trapped in a living nightmare.

The St. Joseph Health Center/Emergency Trauma Center scheduled a seminar on child abuse for March 18 and Lynne decided to go. She returned to announce, "I met Laura Rogers today." Lynne had known about Laura's phone call, but we had not met her yet. Before I had time to tell her about my meeting, she continued. "I went in and sat at a table by myself with my tape recorder. I wanted to be sure I could see everybody who came in. Only a smattering of people were there and this lady walks up and says, 'Are you Lynne Barnhart?' She must have seen my name on the registry.

"I figured somebody might recognize me and my heart started pounding and I said, 'Yes, I am.' I didn't have the faintest idea what to expect."

"'I'm Laura Rogers,' she said, 'and I want you to know you don't have to go through this alone. May I sit with you?' As soon as she said her name, I got tears in my eyes and started to breathe again.

"Laura shared something with me, Keith, that could affect us more than anything I got from the seminar." Lynne's eyes were wide with fear. "There's something called a 'pick up order.' The Division of Family Services can come with the police and take children from the school without the parents' permission and by the time the school notifies the parents, the kids are already gone. Keith, what if the police decide Matthew and Emily aren't safe with us and the DFS and police go to their school and pick them up?"

I just didn't think that was possible until I started reading *The Child Abuse Industry* by Mary Pride. I didn't have to read far to realize that in nearly all cases involving suspected child abuse, children are legally abducted from their homes.

Lynne made arrangements with Matthew and Emily's principal and a mother who lived close to the school so we could snatch our own children away into hiding if necessary. I kept thinking, all these things we have to plan. This is like an underground set up for the protection of our own children. This can't be real! It can't be happening! Here we are, trying to protect our kids from being taken out of our home and I'm completely innocent!

In our monthly church news letter I wrote, "Cast all your anxiety on Him because He cares for you." During the past two months I'd applied this Bible verse more than at any other time in my life. Because we could count on the Lord's

ability and readiness to help, we could refuse to be destroyed
by the nightmare that was enveloping us.

Our trust in God was tested even more a few days later as
Lynne and I sat aghast in front of our TV screen. Although
my name wasn't mentioned again, my case was Channel
Five's feature story of the night. "Charges against a
suspected child abuser are expected to be filed in the next
week or two," reporter Kathy Leonard declared. "Some
parents are getting impatient with the slow moving wheels
of justice."

A picture of our church filled the screen as the TV
reporter's voice picked up the tale. "The Cave Springs Baptist
Church Child Care Center has been under investigation by
St. Charles police since last December." The camera focused
on the playground area with the church in the background.
"Police say seven boys, ages four and five, have told inves-
tigators they were abused at the school, reportedly between
September and December."

The camera panned to a broken, dangling swing set in the
playground, which had recently been replaced. "Parents of
former students want to know why charges haven't been filed
in the case. St. Charles Police Lieutenant Patrick McCarrick
says the investigation isn't complete."

The camera focused on McCarrick as he spoke. "We believe
other employees of the school can tell us things that will help
the investigation [or] at least confirm for us if the suspect
had opportunity to commit the crime. All of our witnesses so
far are four-year-old kids. We need some adult witnesses and
we think there are some available but they refuse to speak
with us."

I ground my teeth in disgust. The implication was that the
Child Care workers had refused to talk, as though they had
something to hide. The real truth was that our attorneys had
advised them not to talk because the police would twist what
they said and use their statements against me.

Reporter Leonard switched to Robert Benjamin, whom she
called a specialist in family law. "He says children are believable witnesses."

Benjamin spoke. "There is clearly no reason why, just
because these children are four year olds, that charges
should not be filed without corroboration of an adult."

Leonard resumed her narration. "While many residents
who live near [the church] wonder why the [Child Care]

Center hasn't been shut down if there is suspicion of child abuse, the Division of Family Services and juvenile courts of St. Charles both say they have no jurisdiction over a church run day care center. They say these centers are exempt from state licensing rules and regulations.

"Officials say there may be no need to close the Center once charges are filled. Some parents of the victims are accusing a St. Charles Baptist minister but charges have not been filed yet."

I looked at Lynne in consternation. The fearful parents, the Division of Family Services, the St. Charles police, the county prosecutors, and Channel Five—it looked as if they were all closing in on me.

They were sending the message that I was guilty.

Guilty with no presumption of innocence.

Chapter Five

Arrested and Jailed

**"As we walked down the hall [of the jail] no one had
to tell me that even the most hardened criminals
detest child molesters."**

It was April and Dad was in the hospital in DeSoto with
pneumonia. Mom told us not to worry, his condition wasn't
serious. If we wanted to come, she would welcome our visit.
We decided to go. It would be nice to get away, even if it was
just for one night.

Budding trees waved lacy green arms as we sped along the
highway. The children quickly curled into their seats and fell
asleep while Lynne and I enjoyed the scenic countryside. I
was the one who broke the silence. "I talked with Charlie this
morning."

"Has he heard anything more about charges being filed?"

"Charlie says DeVouton plans to file something, but some
of the children are still being taken for counseling. He says
there are two more now, making nine boys. He's even mentioned filing charges against some Child Care workers."

"Good grief, and how many counts are they coming up
with?"

"DeVouton is waiting to determine how many children and
all the allegations, then they can determine the number of
counts and file charges. Charlie still doesn't really know
when that might be. He has told the PA, however, that I'll
turn myself in if they file charges."

"Charlie didn't see any problem with you leaving for De-
Soto for the night, then?"

"None at all. I told him we had to be back for you to go to
work tomorrow afternoon. Now let's leave the subject behind
in St. Charles where it belongs. Uh, there's something in the
glove compartment for you, Dear."

Lynne gave me a sideways glance and reached to open the compartment door. I delighted in her smile as she opened the bag and exclaimed, "Why Keith, it's Sandi Patti's newest tape, 'Morning Like This.'"

"I know, I bought it, Dear." I gave her a sly smile. "You said the other day you wanted some different music. Do you like it?"

"Oh, you!" Lynne answered in mocking disgust. "I know you bought it. I'm just so surprised, that's all." Lynne ripped off the cellophane wrapper. "I love Sandi Patti, and I've really been wanting this tape." She pushed it into the tape player.

Sandi's clear strong voice lifted our hearts together in praise to God. Our spirits soared with the music and the anticipation of our overnight reprieve.

We stopped at the hospital and saw Dad on the way into DeSoto. He was feeling fine, he said, and didn't know why he couldn't go home. His snow white crew cut blended with the white pillows making his flushed, ruddy complexion stand out sharply in contrast. His eyes sparkled and his smile welcomed us. I was glad we had come.

We talked about church and Dad's volunteer work at the funeral home. He'd retired twice before, first from being a mechanic 25 years for the Missouri Pacific Railroad, then from his own hardware store after 22 more years. Dad spoke in short phrases divided by long pauses. "Before I forget, Keith—" He coughed a spell before going on. "Will you and Matthew take that winter cover off the air conditioner in the front bedroom window? You'll have to get a ladder and get on the front porch roof to get at it, you know."

"It won't be any problem," I assured him.

He changed the subject and asked questions about my problems. "How'd all this get started anyway? What's it doing to your church? Is there still a chance of arrest?"

I tried to answer his questions. "As far as the arrest goes, I've told my attorney to call me and I'll turn myself in and post bond. I just talked to Charlie this morning. He's checked with the prosecuting attorney and they aren't ready to file charges."

"Well, let's hope not. I can't get out of here yet to sign our house papers for your bond."

"I understand. We'd be in double trouble though, because Virginia Hull's visiting her sister in California so she's not here to sign papers on their house either."

When the nurses brought Dad his supper we decided we'd better leave. "Mom's probably got our supper waiting, Dad. We'll stop by on the way home tomorrow." He smiled contentedly when we left.

Mom did have dinner ready. A huge pot of homemade vegetable soup, followed by fresh baked chocolate cake with thick chocolate frosting. Emily and Lynne helped set the table while Matthew and I played catch. It was only a few minutes before we sat around the table in Mother's big old fashioned kitchen. When the cake was passed, I took my usual slice off the side saying, "Watch carefully, Matthew, this is how it's done."

"Mothers never forget what their sons like, do they, Keith," Lynne said with amusement.

"Fortunately, they don't," I agreed, as I swallowed my first bite. I wondered later in the evening what it was about coming home. Does our sense of security that we feel as children, with Mom and Dad nearby, stay with us all our lives? The tone of Mom's voice mingling with the clatter of dishes in the kitchen brought back memories, and the stacks of books and magazines here and there reminded me how I'd come by my habit of reading. I ate another piece of chocolate cake before hiking up the stairs with Lynne for bed.

"Peaceful, isn't it," I said to Lynne as we sat together at the breakfast table the next morning.

"It certainly is. Why don't we just stay here for a week, or a month, or however long it takes for everything to blow over?" We exchanged understanding smiles. "Well, at least for today," she sighed. "How's that for being realistic?"

Almost before I realized it, the day was half gone. "Come on, Matthew, let's get that air conditioner taken care of."

We walked outside where I watched him climb the ladder. Matthew didn't need a reason to get on the roof.

I came behind, gingerly watching each step. It didn't take long to get the air conditioner cover but while we were up there, a police car came into view. A strange feeling shot through me as it cruised slowly past the house. "Did you see the police car, Matthew?" I asked as we put the ladder away.

"What police car?"

"One drove by while we were on the roof. Probably just their regular beat." For the time I thought nothing more about it.

I packed our bags in the car before going in again. "Lynne, shall we leave now and beat the traffic or wait and go after the rush?" I was having a hard time returning to all the stress.

"It doesn't really matter with me, Keith," Lynne said as she offered me a Pepsi. "You're driving, only I don't know if the traffic ever lets up on Friday nights."

"It's only three," Mother chimed in. "Emily's reading and Matthew's watching TV. Why don't you stay a little longer and let me fix you some supper?"

I didn't really have to be persuaded. We were all sitting in the family room so relaxed we didn't want to move.

The doorbell interrupted our peace.

Emily followed me to the door. "Keith Barnhart?" the uniformed officer asked.

"I'm Keith Barnhart," I replied, knowing intuitively why the officer had come, yet desperately hoping I was wrong.

"I'm sorry," the officer said, "but I have a warrant for your arrest." Emily ran to her mother in the family room the second she heard his words. "We have to take you down to the jail." His words were so irrational. Hadn't I checked with Charlie? The prosecutors had told him they weren't going to file charges yet. He'd told them to call and I'd turn myself in. Why did the St. Charles police decide to have me arrested 50 miles away at my parents' house? If they'd called my attorney and waited a couple of hours I would have turned myself in.

"May I tell my wife?" The officer nodded assent.

I turned and saw Mother already crumpled in a chair crying and shaking her head, "It can't be, it can't be," she kept repeating. "It just can't be."

Emily, white and trembling, had already reached Lynne in the family room. "Mom, they have a warrant for Dad's arrest!"

Lynne rushed to me before I could cross the living room. I saw the terror I felt reflected in her eyes. "We shouldn't be so surprised," I said as I handed her my billfold.

"I'll call Charlie," she said. I embraced her briefly, then turned and left. "Your Bible, Keith." Lynne knew I'd want it but I couldn't turn around.

As I walked out the door I heard Matthew cry, "Mom, what are they doing to Dad?" I heard the fear in his voice, but I had to keep going.

Fragmented thoughts kept colliding in my mind as I

walked down the steps of my parents' home. It had been so peaceful just a few minutes before. Now Mother was crying. How could I say goodbye to Dad in the hospital? How long would I be in jail? My kids were frightened, my wife fearful of the worst. Tomorrow was Saturday, and all the legal offices would be closed. It would be difficult getting things ready to make bond on Monday. I was terrified and relieved only slightly for not being handcuffed.

The officer kept apologizing as I walked with him to the patrol car. I heard the car door slam shut behind me. For a moment I was alone except for the deathly silence of my own fear, then a still small voice echoed in my mind, "The Lord is my light and my salvation; whom shall I fear? The Lord is the defense of my life; whom shall I dread?. . . When I am afraid, I will put my trust in Thee."

Lynne was on the phone to Charlie's office before the police drove out of sight. "I'm calling from DeSoto. Keith's been arrested!"

"He's arrested! When?" the secretary asked.

"Just now. The police have taken him to the DeSoto Jail. We understand he'll be transported later today to St. Charles. What should I do? We've got to get him out!"

"I'll call Charlie and get instructions for you and I'll call the courthouse too and find out about bond. Lynne, I don't want to discourage you, but all the offices close here at five. I'll do what I can but I doubt we can get him out today."

"I know, I understand. I'll wait for you to call back."

Lynne made one other call to St. Charles and in a few minutes, Lea Haney, my secretary phoned. "Lynne, I just heard about Keith. Your house is being searched too. From the report I got, policemen are swarming all over the place, and they're taking out stuffed animals and things like that. I'll go over there and wait until you get home."

As soon as Charlie's office called back Lynne and the children came by the jail. They huddled together in a small knot as an officer stepped forward and slid a key into my cell door. I struggled for control, feeling powerless standing behind bars, shaken at seeing my wife and children crying. Tears streamed down my face too, as I stepped over and hugged each one.

"Were you able to talk to Charlie, Lynne?" She nodded and wiped her face with a tissue.

"I got his office." Lynne swallowed a muffled sob. "He's not in. I'm supposed to call him when I get back to St. Charles. We did find out about the bond." Lynne's lips quivered. "It's $350,000 with no ten percent."

"Three hundred and fifty thousand dollars!" I repeated in shocked dismay. I slumped down on a nearby bench. "Dad's in the hospital and Virginia Hull's out of state, so neither can sign for bond as we planned." I held out my hands, palms up and shook my head. "There's certainly no way we can come up with $350,000." I took off my glasses, pushed my fingers against my throbbing temples and sat for a moment in near despair.

As if to steady me from the first blow, Lynne put her hand on my shoulder. "Lea called and said the police have broken into our house. I've got to go, but right now I can't even remember how to get home. Can you write down the highway numbers?" She dug in her purse and handed me her small notebook and pen.

"We've done all we can to prepare for this," I said when I handed her the instructions. "Apparently our plans are not what God has in mind."

Lynne walked with determined steps as she left the jail with the children trailing behind. She knew she could only do one thing at a time and the most logical move was to get back to St. Charles, contact Charlie, and rely on the support of the church family. As they left the cell block, the officer locked me back in my cell. I felt utterly devastated.

I paced a circle in the cell, then sat down on the hard bunk. I would not be spending the night in DeSoto so there was no mattress. A whispered prayer escaped my lips, "Lord, how in the world can we raise $350,000?"

Eventually two plain clothesmen were brought to my cell by the officer on duty. I recognized detectives Pope and Harvey immediately but their familiar faces gave no comfort. I had not seen them since the night they questioned me. They had come to escort me back to the St. Charles Jail. At Harvey's request, I extended my hands to be handcuffed.

On her way home Lynne tried to encourage Emily and Matthew, recalling ways the Lord had provided for us in the past. "Through all the difficulties we've had, He's never let us down," she declared.

"Mom, how long will Dad be in jail? When can we get to see

him?" Emily's voice was tinged with apprehension.

"Mr. Bridges will do everything he can to get your dad out as soon as possible. I hope that will be tomorrow, but if not—one thing we know for sure, we can't get him out tonight. So we'll pray for him. If only he had his Bible." Lynne's mouth was dry, she was tired, and her shoulders felt pinched in a vise, but she had to keep talking, she had to control her thoughts as well as the children's.

"I don't know how things will work out, but they will, we just have to trust and wait and see what the Lord's going to do," she told them.

"We don't know what we'll find when we get back to the house. We've been prepared for this since December and today's the day. We may have to pick things up and put things away. If the police have taken anything, I'm sure we'll get it back."

Dusk crept across the sky deepening the gloomy atmosphere inside the patrol car. Detective Pope, silent and alone in the front seat, concentrated on driving. I glanced to my left at Detective Harvey and decided he'd make a perfect star for "The Godfather."

"Would you like to talk with me, Keith?" Harvey asked. "It'll be easier if you'll talk." He had not only made up his mind I was guilty; he wanted a confession and would settle for nothing less.

"I tried to talk to you before. You didn't want to hear what I had to say then, why should I talk to you now?" I couldn't help but smile a bit at the humor of his ridiculous assumption.

Harvey's anger exploded in a rush of words. "I'll be glad when the day comes I can see you up the river in [the state prison] Jeff[erson] City!" His adamant voice filled the car as he shifted his weight, turning more my way. "You think this is funny? A big joke?" He jabbed a thick finger in my direction. "I'm going to see you in prison and see how funny you are then!"

He launched into a long lecture, but at least he respected me enough not to swear. We rode in silence then. After awhile I stole a quick glance and saw sulking rage distorting his full face.

I was so naively stupid. In an effort to be polite or conversational or something, I asked, "I understand our house is being searched and I wonder how bad it's going to be for my wife and kids?"

"I don't believe in trashing a house," Harvey grunted. "But your house ought to be trashed anyway; it wouldn't make much difference." I settled into the car seat a bit deeper, refusing to play his game by showing my anger.

At least the car seat was more comfortable than the hard slab in the DeSoto jail. For the remaining miles, only the intermittent chatter of a distant dispatcher broke the silence.

Finally the one hour ride ended. As Detective Harvey opened the door and motioned me out, a fresh wave of fear washed over me making my heart pound frantically and my clammy hands tremble. I stepped handcuffed from the police car into the blinding light of TV cameras. My knees trembled as the two detectives led me to the back door of the jail. As we walked down the hall, no one had to tell me that even the most hardened criminals detest child molesters.

The cell door clanged behind me. At this despairing moment the paradoxical words of King David suddenly came to mind: "Why are you in despair, O my soul? And why have you become disturbed within me? Hope in God, for I shall again praise Him. . . . "

Lynne made only one wrong turn before hitting the rush hour traffic and arrived home just minutes before the evening news. Several church members were already outside.

Lynne pushed a tape into the VCR, then walked through the house. She could tell that every drawer, closet, and book had been gone through.

"Well, I really expected things to be worse, at least everything's not all over the floor," she said. Several well meaning church members were standing around, some with food, others offering to help in any way they could. One of the men was trying to temporarily fix a door frame that had been shattered by the police.

My arrest was the lead story on all the St. Louis TV newcasts that evening. Lynne's anger peaked as she watched Channel Five's Al Naipo standing outside the St. Charles Police Station narrating the events leading up to my arrest: "At this moment the suspect, 40-year-old Keith Barnhart, pastor of Cave Springs Baptist Church, is enroute here. . . . "

"That's pitiful," Lynne fumed with dry-eyed anger as she

stood in front of the TV holding the remote control. "They must have planned to make a special event out of Keith's arrest!"

The camera focused on Chief Prosecuting Attorney William Hannah waiting nearby. "I feel that based on what I can see and the evidence that we have, we will have no problem with the conviction." He spoke with the casual confidence of authority.

Al Naipo picked up the narration. "Two boys came forward during the last two weeks and one of them provided the break in the case."

"There can't be evidence! He didn't do anything!" Lynne vented her exasperation at the TV. Church friends surrounded her protectively, equally enraged.

When Charlie received word from his office that I was arrested, he swung into action. He knew that veteran prisoners understood how the system works. In an attempt to get their own charges dismissed they will call the PA and lie, claiming that the defendant in a high publicity case has confessed his crime in prison. And the one thing Charlie knew for certain, the police and the PA wanted a confession from me.

After the news, Lynne called Charlie. "They've charged him with 15 felony counts including sodomy, sexual abuse, and kidnapping," he reported. "Mrs. Barnhart, a judge has made himself available for tomorrow at noon, so if you can have $350,000 or eight families willing to put up their property for bond at my office by eleven we should be able to get Keith out tomorrow afternoon. I know it's Saturday, but a judge will be there."

"Thank you, Charlie, we'll do it," Lynne answered, not knowing how. "What papers do we need to bring?"

"You'll need descriptions of the deeds or property tax receipts. By the way, what time did the police pick your husband up in DeSoto?"

"Five after three, I wrote it down. Why?"

"That's very interesting, I checked and that's exactly the time they filed for the search warrant. They had it all planned."

"You mean they really did plan to make a media event out of this? But why?"

"They figured to shake him up by arresting him at his parents' home. He didn't expect it and the police probably hoped the shock would lead to a confession. Plus, with you out of town they expected no would be at the house to destroy or hide evidence and they would have a better chance of finding something."

"Charlie, the bond is so high and they're not allowing the 10 percent, is there a connection there too?"

"Most likely." Charlie's steady voice calmed Lynne as he explained the psychological tactics of the police. "With all the publicity, the public wouldn't like anything less, besides, a high bond is more of a statement that the evidence is strong. With bond that high," Charlie continued, "they probably expect to hold him until the trial. Besides, it puts the defense at a disadvantage because he can't be out giving his side of the story nor can he be available to work with me."

"But Charlie, how did they know we were out of town? Only Keith's secretary, Lea, and you knew."

"There's no way of knowing that right now."

When Lynne hung up the phone she turned to Jane Carlson and Irene Dunn, two church women still waiting with her. "Charlie says we need to contact people and see if anybody will put their property up for bail," she explained.

Irene's natural authority from 25 years of teaching school instinctively took over. "With both your front and back doors broken, my husband says you'd better come spend the night with us, Lynne, and as soon as we get home, I'll start calling people."

"I'll call my husband right now," Jane said, "and see if we can put up our house or property." Her call was short and as she put the phone down she remarked, "He didn't need time to make up his mind. 'Sure,' he said. That makes one and only seven more to go."

Matthew went home with Danny, his buddy from church. "You and Emily come on over when you're ready, Lynne," Irene requested. "We'll leave now so I can start calling church members. Once at home, Irene settled herself beside the telephone and started down the church directory list. "Brother Keith's been arrested and the bond's $350,000. We need people to put up their property for bond." Irene filled them in on details, gave them instructions, and added, "There's a special meeting at the church tonight at 8:30. You'll want to be there if you can."

Church members responded to Irene's calls as if she had called "Code Blue." Even though it was a Friday night, within two hours over 40 people had gathered at church to pray and discuss what steps they could take to get me out of jail. Within 20 minutes, 22 homes —more than enough— were made available for bond, and it wasn't even necessary to include the church property.

Confined to the jail, I had no idea what was happening among the church members. I was concerned about what would happen on the inside of the jail walls. I understood I'd be here only temporarily, then moved to the county jail, no comforting thought, because I'd heard hair raising stories about the St. Charles County Jail. I too had concluded my arrest was a staged production, how else would the media be waiting to record it.

Shortly after my arrival, I was taken to a central desk in a cell block area. I saw Detective Pope and the Chief Prosecuting Attorney, Bill Hannah, off by themselves talking. Hannah glanced my way and I wondered if he was checking to see if I'd made a confession.

A woman clerk took my fingerprints; someone else backed me against a wall that faced several cells and took several Polaroid mug shots. Another officer then took my shoes, belt, watch, everything in my pockets, and even my glasses. Then I was locked alone into an empty six by six holding cell. There was no furniture, only a slab jutting out of the wall that served as a bunk.

Eventually the woman at the desk left and I was alone. Each minute seemed an eternity. I tried recalling my childhood and training for the ministry. Was there anything that had prepared me for this? My parents were moral and ethical. At seminary we'd only been instructed to keep the office door open when counseling a woman.

I'd never had anything but respect for the law nor even so much as a traffic ticket. I had read about a child abuse case or two in the St. Louis area and was vaguely aware of the horrendous McMartin child abuse case in California. Still, I wasn't aware of the wave of hysteria and disaster sweeping the nation in it's wake.

It would be months before I learned that the bureaucracy set up to protect children actually allows state social workers, mental health professionals, law enforcement officers, attorneys, and allied professionals to accuse almost anyone of child sexual abuse. Guilt is established on the basis of an accusation and innocence must be proven. I was totally unaware that this was the devastating trap I was caught in.

The cement slab bed was hard so I stood and stretched. Time seemed to stop. I rubbed my fingers over my wrist, feeling only a slight square-shaped indention where my watch had been. Being without my glasses put my whole world out of focus, adding to my already disoriented feelings. There was absolutely nothing to do but wait. After what seemed to be a very long time, I wondered if everyone had forgotten me.

Finally a patrolman returned, unlocked my cell, and escorted me to the booking desk where I was given my possessions. I put my glasses on and peered at my watch. I'd been in the St. Charles City Jail just two hours.

"Your hands, please." The patrolman clicked on my second set of 'cuffs for the day, escorted me to his patrol car, and transported me to the old St. Charles County Jail. There I had to go through the booking process all over again.

"I didn't know we're fingerprinted each time we're moved," I commented to the kind young lady who was handling the job. "First time going through this you learn a lot."

"For the first time, you're doing very well." Her voice was warm and her smile sweet and neither seemed tainted by professional indifference.

"I've had a lot of time to pray this afternoon, and it's just by the strength of the Lord I'm able to hold up."

"Take everything off except your glasses and put your things in here, then put these on," a deputy instructed. He handed me a brown paper bag, slippers, and a bilious orange jump suit. Until then I'd never realized black and white stripes were out.

Before being taken to my cell I was allowed to call Lynne. "It's me, Dear, how are you doing?"

"Thank God, I'm O.K. Are you all right?"

"Sure. What's happening? How are the kids?"

"Matthew's over at Danny's and Emily and I are getting ready to go to the Dunns for the night. The police did search the house."

"I'm not surprised. What all did they do to it?"

"The frame on the back door is broken. After I started looking around we could tell they'd been through everything, but it's not what I'd call trashed."

When I asked about prospects for bond, Lynne told me about the judge available for the next day. "Irene is making calls now and we have some property already." Lynne talked so fast I could hardly keep up with her. "People are meeting at the church tonight, and we'll all meet Charlie at his office tomorrow at eleven. If all goes well, you'll be out tomorrow afternoon."

"I sure hope so," I said without any assurance that the extremely high bond could be made. When I hung up the phone, I wondered what would happen between now and the next afternoon.

In the back of my mind I remembered reading about two men who had recently been arrested for the abduction and rape of a girl in a nearby suburb. Some of the inmates had jumped up and down on the guy and really worked him over. I refused to think about what could happen to me, an accused child molester.

"Reverend, we're going to put you in with Randy, he's a Christian." The courteous deputy led me into a block of four cells. He explained that the inmates had free run of the block until being locked up two to a cell later that night. Not quite knowing what to think, I sat down on a thin pad that covered a steel bed that extended from the wall like a shelf.

Randy was a lanky fellow who looked to be in his mid-twenties. "Must be a pretty hard time for you," he sympathized. He introduced me to another inmate. "This is Paul, he's a Christian too. Let's all have prayer right now." Without telling me anything about his circumstances, Randy bowed his head and started praying. I sat amazed. Rather than being attacked, I was being prayed for. After praying, Randy pulled a box out from under his bed. "Thought you might like to use this tonight," he said, and handed me a Bible. I felt like God had sent an angel.

The inmates in the cell block were viewing the NCAA basketball tournament on a television wired up just outside the cell. The game ran late, so it was 10:30 p.m. before the evening news came on. I stepped closer to the TV and watched myself walk handcuffed into jail.

"That's me," I said, viewing myself with detached emotion. I saw one of the inmates roll his eyes and realized I should have kept my mouth shut and not drawn attention to myself.

"YOU must really be something," the man sneered. I felt

more secure when the deputy came into the block and locked Randy and me into our cell for the night. My hard bed yielded no comfort and my troubled thoughts kept sleep at bay.

It was nearly eleven that evening when Lynne finally drove into the Dunns' driveway. Irene told her that more than enough people had pledged their homes for bond.

Once Lynne had Emily in bed, Lynne opened her Bible and sat down beside her. "I have this verse, Dear, it's been my favorite verse for a long time. You read it."

Lynne slid her Bible close to our blue-eyed daughter and put her finger at the beginning of the passage. Emily voiced the words softly.

". . . We are afflicted in every way, but not crushed, we're perplexed but not despairing, persecuted but not forsaken, struck down but not destroyed." Emily stopped and looked trustingly to her mother for an explanation.

"Emily, these are real life things that happen to people and they're happening to us now." Lynne was speaking for her own encouragement as well. "The Lord will not allow severe consequences to touch His children. We're not being crushed, we are not." Lynne's patient voice was strong with conviction. "We're going to be knocked around a lot but nothing will destroy us. God will only let it go so far."

Breakfast in the jail came at 6:30 and if you chose to eat, you ate then. I discovered the inmates saved their styrofoam cups, filling them with enough coffee to last until the next meal. But cold coffee didn't excite me, so I inspected the showers. I decided I was better off waiting to clean up until I got home.

Randy and I visited some. "I'm just now beginning to understand about God and salvation and all," he shared. "In fact, it's just been since being here that I've asked God's forgiveness and invited Him into my life."

I spent a good part of the morning by myself, reading Randy's Bible and praying. After lunch I played chess with one of the inmates, and listened to Christian programs on another inmate's radio in an attempt to push away the persistent fear that my bail arrangements might have fallen through.

I needn't have worried. About 50 church members and other supporters were at the court house by eleven waiting for Charlie Bridges. He led them through the large double doors and into a hallway. Irene Dunn's husband, Troy, had recently had back surgery, but he came anyway and balanced on crutches back near the doors.

The police had apparently already tipped the St. Louis media to anticipate my release on bond. Vans from the three St. Louis network TV stations pulled into the parking lot. Al Naipo, the reporter from Channel Five, came barging through the double doors, shoving Troy off balance. Friends nearby jumped to his rescue and kept him from falling.

"Hey, you almost knocked a crippled man to the floor," Ida Smith shouted.

Naipo glared back at the petite little grandmother. "This is a free country. I'm entitled to get in."

"We know that," Ida said. "We just wish you would tell the whole truth."

"They seem to be a fact of life," Ida muttered, not ashamed to show her disgust. "We can hardly take the Child Care children out to play anymore 'cause Channel Five keeps their van parked across the street half the time. It's just not right exposing the children that way."

Charlie's arrival brought quick smiles. Ignoring the TV people, he quickly sorted deeds and tax receipts brought by the church members. Then he directed them to Judge William Lohmar's office. It took until almost two to complete the bond posting process. Then en masse, the crowd of supporters walked the two blocks to the county jail and waited expectantly outside. The TV reporters had already driven over.

"Reverend Keith Barnhart?" I jumped when the deputy called my name. "Your bond's been posted." I silently breathed a prayer of thanks. What had seemed impossible had happened.

He turned the key in the cell door. I stepped out and took the paper bag that contained my clothes. After making a hurried change, I walked back to the desk where I had been fingerprinted and signed papers pledging that I would not talk to any of the accusing children or parents. If I did so, the documents warned, my bond could be revoked. I was now free to go.

I opened the door to cheers and loud applause from the crowd of supporters who had made possible my bond. Suddenly I saw Lynne. We ran into each other's arms and embraced.

Arms clasped tightly around each other, Lynne and I turned to face the group, ignoring the omnipresent cameras pressing toward us. I struggled to maintain composure, fighting back tears of joy.

"Thank you. Thank you all for making my freedom possible." My throat was too tight to say more. I could only smile and wave. Tears streamed down my face and I struggled to control my emotions as I scanned the familiar faces who were there to say they believed in me. It was one of the most emotional experiences of my life.

Chapter Six

Arraigned and Sustained

"As we walked inside the courthouse, a small mob rushed at us from both sides."

After my release on bond, Lynne and I picked Emily and Matthew up at a friend's house. We were all happy to get back. It even felt good to be almost knocked down by Jackson's exuberant welcome. The four of us were content to spend a quiet evening at home enjoying each other's company.

Saturday morning, the *St. Louis Post-Dispatch* brought me back to reality. There was a big story on the allegations against me, which quoted both my attorney and Lieutenant McCarrick.

Lieutenant McCarrick: "All of the boys identified their abuser as Barnhart. . . . Besides the physical evidence, authorities also have evidence from psychologists saying that the children's behavior was 'consistent with kids who have been sexually abused.'" McCarrick also claimed that "employees at the Center have been uncooperative with police."

Charlie Bridges: "There's nothing to support the allegations, none of the adults out there are supporting what the children are saying."

Sunday morning my photo shared the front page with Jim Bakker's. "Lynne, this is awful," I groaned. "People will see me as they do Bakker."

I determined that as long as I had the support of my congregation I would continue preaching. However, in order not to damage the reputation of the Christian school our children attended I decided to take a leave of absence from the school's Board of Fathers.

We didn't know what to expect at the church that Sunday

morning. As we pulled into the church parking lot, we saw a
lone picket holding a silent warning. But the attendance was
up dramatically and everything went well during the services.

Ida called me at home early Monday morning. "Brother
Keith, we've got a picket out here who is acting crazy." Ida
was both frightened and irritated.

"Is he the same one that was at the church yesterday?"

"I don't know, but he follows the cars down the driveway
yelling at the parents, telling them we abuse children, and
they shouldn't bring their kids here. He follows them right
up to the door. Brother Keith, he's even tried to get in the
Child Care. I had to walk right up to him and tell him to 'get
outa' here.' The parents are scared to take the children out
of their cars. We don't think you'd better come to church this
morning. No telling what he might do if he sees you."

I waited about an hour and called my secretary, Lea. "I
guess I'd better not come over until later."

"I agree, Brother Keith. When I came in a few minutes ago
there were two police cars, that picket, and about four other
people outside. On top of that, a woman just threatened us
over the phone. She wanted to know if this 'hell hole' was
closed. She wouldn't give her name but said I would be
hearing from her because she was going to come over and see
that the Child Care was shut down. For everyone's safety, I
went through and locked every door in the church."

After talking with Lea, I called Charlie. "Keep the doors
locked from now on," he advised. We agreed the safety of the
children was our main concern.

Intermingled with the heckling and threatening phone
calls came a steady number of encouraging calls from well
wishers and friends. Wayne Dismuke, a youth minister who
attended Southwest Baptist University in Bolivar, Missouri
where I had been student body president, called shortly after
my arrest. "I've heard about your troubles from some of our
college buddies, news travels fast. I felt uncomfortable con-
tacting you right out of the blue, Keith. I just couldn't bring
myself to believe that you had done these terrible things."

"I understand, Wayne. It's such a horrible thing that most
people think there must be some truth in it for the allegations
to even get started."

"Keep me informed on what's happening and I'll pass the
word around. Believe me, Keith, you've got our trust and

support." What would I do without friends, I thought, as I put the phone back in it's cradle.

I phoned my colleague, Harold Hendrick. "Would you consider calling a ministers conference for prayer and support on my behalf and invite the media?"

Harold readily agreed. "Excellent idea. I'll set it up for tomorrow morning at your church, Keith." In less than 24 hours nearly 50 ministers gathered at the church with a number of reporters present.

"The old saying is that where there's smoke, there's fire," I told the group. "That's the thing that probably first came to your mind. I assure you I didn't start the fire, nor do I know how the fire started. I just wish they'd quit blowing smoke my way." The ministers stirred slightly and smiled. I heard a few scattered chuckles.

"I must tell you that the church has been totally supportive from the very beginning. In fact, last Sunday, after my arrest, we had a 40 per cent increase in attendance. I sure hope I don't have to get arrested every weekend to get attendance like that.

"We've been as open with our people as we can and the workers who are closest to the investigation have said from the very beginning, not only could it not have happened, it did not happen. I believe that at some point, they will be able to share their testimonies.

"My attorney says it could be six months to a year before this comes to trial. I hope you will continue to wait with us and pray for us."

I shared verses from Psalms 27 that comforted me. "God is my salvation, my defender, and my deliverer. . . . Wait for the Lord; be strong, and let your heart take courage; yes, wait for the Lord."

Harold gave a statement to the press. "Even if he were guilty, which we don't believe he is, we would still want to minister to him as we would any time one of our own gets wounded. We want everyone to recognize that something like this could happen to any of us. We're not trying to cover up sexual abuse, but we don't want the community to condemn Barnhart when he has not been proven guilty. All we're asking is that he have his day in court."

Jim Rogers introduced himself to me at the ministers conference. "My wife, Laura, spoke with you over the phone. We're interested in seeing that you get a fair trial."

"Thank you," I replied, sensing he wasn't entirely convinced of my innocence. "My wife told me about meeting Laura at the St. Joseph Health Center seminar on child abuse."

He invited Lynne and me to their house. "We'd like to know more about your situation, Brother Keith."

Jim later confessed, "I had thought all along that if seven boys were all saying the same thing, like the police and papers said, and the children had not been allowed to be in contact with each other to contaminate their stories, then you certainly must be guilty. But after hearing you speak to the pastors I thought there was a strong possibility you were being railroaded."

We began visiting regularly with the Rogers in their home. We found them to be a resource center on everything to do with families in Missouri. Laura Rogers had served as lobbyist in our state legislature for over 15 years for child and parent concerns and she founded and directed the National Association of Parents and Children.

Through the Rogers I met Terry Gannon, Missouri director of VOCAL, a national organization supporting victims of child abuse laws. I already knew about VOCAL from reading Dr. Larry Speigel's book, *A Question of Innocence*. After attending the first VOCAL meeting I said, "Terry, all these people, I can't believe it, and they're all in the same boat." Both Terry and the Rogers began channeling articles and books my way. Not all the information was encouraging.

We kept running into the statement, "Children don't lie about these things." We'd heard it from the police, the pickets, and now the line began appearing in the media. Chief Prosecuting Attorney Hannah had apparently bought into it. "I'm totally convinced that our evidence is sufficient to convict Barnhart," he said in the *Post-Dispatch*. "I wouldn't have charged him if I hadn't been convinced of that."

My arraignment was coming up in a week. I stopped by to see Charlie. "I see in the media where Hannah says he may personally face off with you in the courtroom."

"That may be to your advantage," Charlie answered with a twinkle in his dark eyes. "He's only personally tried one case and he didn't do too well with it. On the other hand, DeVouton may be the man. He's assigned to your case right now."

"What if I'm convicted, even though I'm innocent? How

much of a sentence could I get?"

Charlie reached for a pad and did some quick figuring. "Well, if you're declared guilty on all of the charges, your minimum sentence would be over a hundred years." He managed a wry smile. "But I don't think that's going to happen. Anyway, we've got to get the preliminary hearing out of the way first. That will come some time after you're arraigned."

Charlie introduced me to his new partner, Bill Seibel. "Bill will represent you at the arraignment. He's practiced law for 15 years, nine of those as assistant prosecuting attorney for St. Charles County. So he knows his way around." Bill Seibel was as animated as Charlie was quiet. He was tall, large framed, with graying hair. They made an interesting team.

Later that evening when the TV news was over and the children were in bed, I told Lynne about my visit with Charlie and Bill Seibel. "Bill will represent me at my arraignment this week. We can't get police or medical records until the preliminary hearing. Charlie doesn't know when that will be yet. So to a great extent, we're operating in the dark."

Lynne had just given Jackson his evening bone. We both stopped and laughed at the game he played before he got down to the business of eating it.

"Charlie has talked to some of the Child Care workers. He's looked around the church and believes I'm innocent. Seibel has done neither yet. I think he's open minded but he needs some hard facts. He did say we've got a complicated case because the children are so young and because there are seven of them.

"On the other hand, Siebel says DeVouton has a reputation of being fast to file charges, and for him to wait four months suggests he must have a weak case. Seibel thinks the prosecution conveyed that to the police and the police went to the media and sicked them on the prosecutor's office creating bad publicity. The media is presenting the picture that these are strong cases and the prosecutor is sitting on them doing nothing.

"That partly explains why they made such a big-to-do about your arrest." Lynne leaned forward, startled by a new thought. "Keith, they're playing political games and your whole future's at stake!"

"Well, yes, it sort'a looks that way."

"Do you realize how much our lives are being altered,

Keith?" Lynne suddenly became teary. I noticed it because it's so unusual for her.

"What do you mean, Dear," I asked. I'd learned to be sensitive to her emotionally, not because she's emotional. It's just that I'm annoyingly stable. I waited a moment then gently prodded. "Are you referring to something specific, Lynne?"

"Yes, it's hard being a pastors wife. I have to keep up with everything. I have to be at church, teach Sunday School, be in the nursery. Keith, it's hard for me to even go in the nursery now." Lynne leaned over and scratched Jackson behind the ears and talked to him. He looked at her with his big liquid eyes, grateful for the attention. "I can hardly stand going in the nursery, especially the pre-schoolers'." Jackson's tail flopped as though giving her sympathy.

"Keith, I love children, and now I can hardly stand hearing one of the little kids say, 'I have to go potty.' I think, O.K., but there's never a time when I'm in that bathroom with a kid that I don't say to myself, 'I hope they can wipe themselves.'

"Little Mark had to go last week and I went into the bathroom with him. I asked if he needed help and he chirped, 'My mom said that nobody's s'posed to touch me down there and if anybody does, I'm s'posed to tell her.' Then he just looked at me. Keith, I'm a nurse, and I sent him home with a dirty bottom. It makes me angry that my feelings towards children have changed so much."

Lynne looked down at Jackson. He'd gone back to his bone. "Maybe I should be a vet's assistant," she said. His tail made one hard thump.

At 1:30 Thursday afternoon following my arrest on Friday, Bill Seibel and I walked together up the hill from his and Charlie's office to the domed St. Charles County Courthouse. It had always reminded me of the U.S. Capitol. I wasn't surprised to see Channel Five encamped outside. I'd come to think of their black cameras as vultures circling, waiting for the kill.

"The arraignment is the first court appearance," Bill explained. "Sometimes the court will read the charges, but we often waive the reading and then the judge gives us the next court date or preliminary hearing date. It's usually just a mere formality."

I looked over at the media and the gathering crowd and managed a thin grin at Bill's comment.

As we walked inside the courthouse a small mob rushed at us from both sides. Police and deputies struggled to hold them back but there was no barrier to shield me from the angry yells and curses hurled by prosecuting parents and their friends. An older man even gave me a shove as I walked by.

Judge William Lohmar presided at the arraignment and imposed a ban barring me from the Child Care Center. His ruling was really unnecessary. I had not gone downstairs since the allegations started, although there was no way I could stop someone from saying, "I saw him downstairs," or "I saw him with a child." It bothered me more that because of the charges against me, the Child Care would soon have to close.

I tried to figure out what each of the seven counts meant, but the language was pretty technical and I wasn't as concerned about the legalities as I was about the stories becoming even more bizarre. One child had even said I went into a house and put him in the bathtub and cut myself and put blood on him. The professionals believed all of this because "children don't lie about these things."

When we left the courthouse Bill remarked, "The hostility in there reminds me of the lynch mobs in the old Frankenstein movies I saw when I was a kid. You know, where the mob comes at the end of the movie with torches, stones, and clubs to get the monster. No disrespect, Reverend, but that's the way these people really look at you—as a monster who needs to be strung up."

Although I no longer went downstairs, Dora and other workers who attended our church stopped by my office quite often. "We've lost a few more children this week, Brother Keith," Dora informed me. "Our attendance is now way less than half."

"With all the rumors going around I guess we can't be too surprised. My attorney told me you and I are being accused of taking these kids on rides, shopping, and even to private homes."

"I don't know how we did all that." Dora's voice was sharp with surprise. "We've never even been in the same car with each other. I guess I shouldn't be shocked by anything after hearing I chased one boy around with a chain saw." Dora sat shaking her head. "We don't even own one."

The Child Care workers had become increasingly concerned for everyone's safety. Ida expressed their common feelings: "Who's to say what these people might do. They're angry, that's for sure." Her forehead, smooth for her age, creased with worry. "They've painted your house, Brother Keith. We've been threatened. Who's to say they won't come and lob a bomb in here?" On March 29 we decided for the safety of the children to close the Child Care by the end of the week.

Ida had taught little children over 22 years, Sandy and Verna around 18, and Marla close to 13 years. They, along with the other workers who had less experience, knew that if I was convicted, they might be too. Anybody who knew them realized how much they were crushed by the false accusations made by parents of children they loved.

Mildred, a grandmother and widow in our church, opened her home for a prayer meeting for the Child Care workers. The time they spent praying together became more beneficial than group therapy as they shared their hurts and concerns and comforted each other with Bible promises.

"It seems as if there's a psalm to fit every occasion," one of the workers commented. "When one of us is down, the others are up."

"We laugh and cry and pray together," Cindy said, "and we remember what you tell us, Brother Keith. 'We can't become bitter against God, and we must pray for the families.'"

Books and articles from the Rogers', VOCAL, and others interested in my case were stacking up. At night after the children were in bed, Lynne and I read and discussed some eye-opening statements.

"Lynne, listen to this," I said, holding up Dr. Lee Coleman's article in *Opinion*. He says that the sacred principle of being assumed innocent before being proven guilty has been abandoned in cases of alleged child sexual abuse. I quoted directly from the text:

"'The single most important reason the system is doing a terrible job at getting at the truth . . . is the direct importation into investigations and court proceedings of the idea that 'children don't lie about sexual abuse. . . .'"

"Keith, isn't that the assumption on which the police are basing their whole investigation?"

"Yes. Now, listen to this. 'Where did . . . . investigators get such an idea? From the 'experts'. . . . The leading lights from psychiatry, psychology, and social work are training investigators to believe that when it comes to alleged sexual abuse, the child's statements are unimpeachable. Ignored at such workshops is the fact that the experts developed their ideas by studying incest in intact families, while the major arena of false allegations [of sexual child abuse] is divorce/custody battles. In the former the child may be pressured to drop a true accusation, but in the latter the pressure may go the other way—to remember something that never happened. The young child may easily be led to the point of sincerely believing in things that did not take place.'"

"Who is this Dr. Coleman anyway?"

"He's identified as a Berkeley psychiatrist and author of the book, *The Reign of Error*. He goes on to say that child protection agencies send children to 'therapy' before any thorough investigation has been done. He also says therapists and investigators believe if a child denies abuse it merely indicates 'yuckky secrets' are hard to tell and the child has been threatened into silence."[1]

"So what he's saying," Lynne concluded, "is that kids can be taken to a place such as the Sexual Abuse Management unit over at Cardinal Glennon Hospital on the basis of an allegation by anyone. And if a child denies anything, it's assumed he's been threatened and is afraid to talk. A well meaning therapist can then lead them into saying anything and because 'children never lie about sexual abuse' you can end up behind bars."

"That's what it sounds like. By accepting the premise of the 'experts,' the police felt they had no choice but to believe them over me."

I continued reading from Dr. Coleman's article. "'When it comes to a child's statement about sexual victimization, there are not two possibilities, lying or telling the truth—but three. A child may be neither lying nor telling the truth. A child, particularly a very young one, may say what he or she believes is true, even though it is not the truth.'"[2]

"Here's an article by William D. Slicker, an attorney in Florida, that's loaded with documentation," Lynne said. "He cites two researchers who say that suggestion is the 'one factor [which] more than anything else' . . . can 'devastate memory and play havoc with our best intended recollection.'"[2]

"Lynne, both Charlie and Bill are coming over to church tomorrow to look around. I'll show them these articles."

I had the articles on my desk when the attorneys arrived. I decided to wait until they finished their inquiry before showing them the entry.

"Today what we really want to do," Charlie said, "is to go through the kids' stories and see how they say the incidents occurred." He put his brief case on the corner of my desk, opened it, and pulled out a yellow pad. "I assume this is your office and I assume it's where they say some of the molestation occurred?" His low steady voice belied his straightforward questioning.

We went over the allegations and events from the beginning, then I asked, "Do you know all of the names of the children accusing me?"

"No." Bill Seibel explained, "Legally, we have no way to get information before a trial. The prosecution knows the more information they give to the defendant's attorney, the longer the preliminary hearing, and it's not a benefit to them to give that information to us now."

Charlie asked about the teachers' schedules and who else might be around the church. He wanted to know Lea's hours too. I also gave them my schedule for the past several months.

"How long does it take by car to get from the church to your home?" Bill asked.

"It's just three miles. I can do it in six to ten minutes, sometimes less."

"I'm not saying you did, but let's assume you took a child to your house. Let's say you had to try to do that today. Let's say the school was functioning. Would it be possible to walk a child out of here without anybody seeing you?"

"I'll let you decide that," I said. I took the attorneys downstairs. "This room we call the Fellowship Hall, the children play, eat, and nap in here. The rooms on the outer perimeter are classrooms and the doors are always open. You can see that it's impossible for anybody to take a child out without one or more of the workers being aware of it."

My attorneys looked around a bit more before we returned to my office and before Bill sat down, he carefully scanned the walls. "I don't want to offend you by what I'm about to say, honestly, 'cause I think it's a perfectly innocent thing, but I've been a prosecutor for nine years and I know how they think." Bill was looking at a poster my secretary had given me that had a diapered baby beside a messy stack of books and papers. It read, "A messy desk is the mark of genius."

"If I was the prosecutor and came in here with a search warrant, I'd take this poster and hop on the jury with it as evidence to discredit your character, and say that you like little boys. It's an innocent poster that lots of people have, but my advice is take it down just in case because I think it could be misinterpreted."

"Yes, of course," I gulped, making a note to go through my whole office. Then I remembered something I needed to ask. "By the way, Marianna Riley from the *St. Charles Post* called and wanted to do a personal profile on me. I told her I wanted to talk to you first."

"No," Charlie answered. "She'll take something down and the prosecutors will subpoena her and they'll get her records, every note she takes. If she writes something down where you say no—"

Bill picked up the thought, "Every time I've dealt with reporters they get at least one thing incorrect. They deal with every topic you can think of and—I've seen a newspaper article when I know something about it and—."

"Yeah," I agreed, "you usually find something, 'Hey this isn't right or this wasn't quoted right.' It amazes me how careful I have to be about every word I say to anybody anymore. I have to be suspicious of everyone I don't personally know."

"And the prosecutor will be looking for every mistake you've ever made," Charlie added, "because he'll want to use that when you testify.

"The problem with this type of case," Charlie continued, "is that they've got seven kids saying, 'You're the one that did it.' And you've already heard it, everyone says, 'if there's that many of them, then you must be guilty.'"

"Charlie, Lynne and I have begun gathering resource material," I said, pointing out some of the most revealing statements from the articles Lynne and I read the night before. "I understand it's after the kids have been to the police, therapists, and other experts, that it's not a question of whether something happened, but what happened. The professionals are not looking to see whether I did something, but what I did. And according to one of these articles, when it comes to questioning the children, anything goes."

I reached for a tape of Dr. Coleman's and Mary Pride's book, *The Child Abuse Industry.* "Coleman is a little hard to listen to but I hope you'll take the time. And Mary Pride's book will startle you. I turned to a marked page where she had quoted Douglas J. Besharaov, former head of the National Center on Child Abuse and Neglect: "The present child protection system is like a 911 emergency phone call system that cannot distinguish between a murder in progress and littering."[3]

"We're happy to accept any information you find that will help your case," Charlie said as he took the materials from me.

We talked about legal fees. "We charge $65 an hour whether one or both of us are working. Because of so many victims, it's going to be time consuming and we're going to need investigators to help us," Charlie explained.

"And what kind of fees can we expect from them?"

"If we get a psychiatrist, he'll be pretty expensive. We'll also have a lot of depositions, especially of the police." That surprised me and I asked for an explanation.

"What happens is the police come up with a final statement from the victims which they've edited from their notes. Unfortunately, some policemen aren't very truthful. They report only what they want to so we want to get the depositions before they destroy their notes.

"We know how they operate in the prosecutor's office too," Bill explained. "They determine who they think is guilty and the prosecutor feels they are doing right by not investigating information that's helpful to the defense."

Charlie and Bill had both worked in the prosecutor's office. They had to know the assumptions under which prosecuting attorneys worked. I felt betrayed by the police and prosecutors I'd always trusted. It was a hard lesson to learn.

We considered a change of venue. "It might be to your advantage to stay here," Charlie pointed out. "You've got a strong support system and people aren't as shocked by the charges."

Bill agreed with Charlie. "That's not just this type of charge, that's true of any charge. It's always easier to get convictions in a rural area."

"The preliminary hearing is now set for June 3. It's purpose is for the judge to determine probable cause," Charlie explained. "In other words, is there cause enough to believe something may have happened?"

Charlie started to put his note pad away and I glanced at my watch. "It's nearly noon already. I have one more question, if you fellows have time?" Charlie nodded.

"I have some friends ready to set up a legal defense fund. Do you have any suggestions along that line?"

"A separate account would be good, for the sake of records," Charlie said.

"I'm not going to pin you down, just an estimate of legal cost."

"A minimum of $10,000. It depends on how long it goes and how much you can pay. Even if I represent somebody and they can't afford to pay, I don't go into court unprepared, because it's my reputation. Bill and I always go prepared."

"When you set up this defense fund," Bill urged, "you've got to stress to people that the other side has all the finances of the city, county, and state. They have the whole police force to investigate you."

"Yes, and they don't have any restrictions on experts they can pay, or deposition costs," Charlie added as he snapped his case shut.

I started walking them to the door. "In other words, I'm being prosecuted by my own tax money." The bitter irony of that remained with me long after they left.

The first of April, Charlie notified me that he planned to contact Dr. Lee Coleman to ask him to get involved in my case. At that time I told Charlie we were planning to visit Lynne's family in New Orleans, April 11-18.

"Just notify your church insurance lawyer, James Whaley first. By the way, I found out today that Chief Prosecutor Hannah told John DeVouton and their secretaries not to tell me that they were planning your arrest."

Being back in New Orleans was great. Lynne's family laughed and hugged a lot and it was good to see Lynne relax, despite her father's debilitating condition. By this time the family was pretty certain that Mr. Blackman had Alzheimer's Disease.

It was the first time we'd seen any of her family since the first allegations were made, but even out of state we couldn't escape harassment. Lea, my secretary called to say that "Fag Go to Hell" had been spray painted on several exterior walls and on two doors of the church. Then she added, "Paul Stevens, along with Tim Raymond Gaylord, and his sister came over to the church when members were there working, and hugged Brenda McDuff [one of the Child Care workers]. None of the children acted afraid."

Leaving New Orleans for St. Charles was terribly hard, especially for Lynne. Her mom was never the type to cry, but she did then; she just sobbed when we pulled away. "I want to get on a space ship for Mars," Lynne stammered, struggling to control her emotions. "First Baptist, Mars would be just fine. Do you think they would call you as pastor?"

Jackson licked our hands when we picked him up from the kennel, and our church family still expressed their love. I called Charlie and found out the status of things. "Dr. Coleman can come," he said. "His fee is $150 per hour and $1,500 a day as a trial witness." We decided to engage his services.

By April 27 the weather had warmed enough for me to enjoy a game of golf again with my close friend, Ben Dole, from the church. Ben's lighthearted temperament and outgoing personality, so different from mine, was the magnet that had drawn us together, and because of our mutual commitment to the Lord's work, we'd developed a deep friendship.

Ben came directly to the golf course after seeing his doctor about chest pain. "Guess it's nothing to worry about. My EKG showed nothing so I'll play a few holes anyway." But he lasted only the first hole and went home.

It was still dark the next morning when I heard the broken voice of Sarah Dole over the answering machine. I reached for the phone beside the bed to interrupt the recording. "There's no easy way to tell you this," she said. "Ben has had a heart attack and just died."

"I'll be there as soon as I can," I assured.

No matter what my personal situation, my life as a pastor and a friend of a bereaved family had to go on.

Chapter 7

Bound Over for Trial

"When would this craziness end?"

Early one Sunday morning I was leafing through the *St. Louis Post-Dispatch*. A bold print type head, "When A Child Points The Finger," jumped out at me. I quickly scanned the article. "Hey Lynne," I called, as I walked to the breakfast table, "Listen to this."

I read to her a challenging quote from the psychiatrist, Dr. Coleman: "'Child protective agencies must quit focusing on only what the child says and start looking at how they investigate such cases. . . . The confusion of mental health specialists is triggered by failure to come to grips with the psychological manipulation of children.'

"And get this quote from a Dr. Vandenberg, a psychologist in Kansas: 'Years ago, prosecutors didn't find child abuse when it was there; now they are finding it when it's not there.'"[4]

Lynne shared my elation. "It's nice to know there are a few professionals around who know what's really going on." We continued to scan articles and research references looking for clues that might unravel the invisible net I was tangled in.

In May, three pastors, Harold Hendrick, Gary Robnett, and Marion Furgerson along with our layman friend, Jim Rogers, formed an ad hoc committee with a threefold purpose: to provide a perspective on my case not available in the media; to solicit prayer for me, my family, and our church; and to request contributions to a legal defense fund.

These four men had no hard evidence of my innocence. They asked the same questions I did. Why were the children saying these things? What physical and emotional evidence were the professionals finding? Why did this evidence point to me? These men were putting themselves and their reputations on the line for me.

They released an appeal letter on May 21: "... We [the ad hoc committee] not only believe that Keith should have his day in court, but that those who know and love him should rally to his support in this time of extreme need." The first gifts for the defense fund soon began arriving.

Lynne's sister, Leanna, made arrangements to leave her three small children with her husband and fly up from New Orleans for the preliminary hearing. She was looking forward to "signing" the hymns in deaf language during the next Sunday's service–a feature which our people always enjoyed. Leanna was already on her way when Charlie called to say the date for the hearing had been extended.

"Oh, no," I sighed. Having been kept in the dark for nearly six months, we had been anxiously waiting to get our hands on all the official reports so we could find out what was going on.

"Did DeVouton say why he's delaying the hearing?" I asked Charlie.

"DeVouton told the judge he's going to file amended charges on you and also file charges against the Child Care workers and other people."

When would this craziness end?

"If they file charges on Lynne, can you represent us both?"

Charlie assured me he could and promised, "I'll let you know as soon as another date is set."

Lynne was disappointed at the delay and concerned about the possibilities of charges that might include other people— "but I'm learning not to be surprised at anything," she said.

Leanna's arrival brightened up our home scene, especially for the children who were feeling the pressure we were under. One afternoon Lynne called me to the kitchen window. "You've gotta see this. Look out there."

Leanna was playing ball with Matthew and Emily. About half the time, Jackson caught the ball first and they had to catch him to get it. As we stood and laughed together, I remembered the first time I met Leanna. It was when Lynne and I had been set up for a blind date. After timidly knocking on the Blackman's door I stood waiting nervously. When a young lady answered the door, I said, "Hi, I'm Keith Barnhart."

"You mus' be ma sista's date," she shot back with a look of

disdain on her face. "You jus' git away from ma sista'," she screeched. "I don' want you 'round heah, you jest git away." Then she stepped back and slammed the door in my face.

I stood there turning red, trying to decide what to do next when the door opened revealing both sisters doubled over with laughter.

"You'll have to excuse my sister, Leanna," Lynne said as she stepped forward and introduced herself. "She's just played Prissy in 'Gone With the Wind'—her high school play, and hasn't recovered yet." Before the evening ended, I realized I'd experienced first hand the "character" of the Blackman family. Leanna was a riot.

Peals of laughter from our back yard pulled me back from the past. "The kids sure enjoy your sister, Lynne. I'm so glad she could be here for the week."

Later in the evening the three of us sat and visited. "Leanna, one of the hard things for Matthew and Emily," Lynne confided, "is that they can't have any friends visit."

"Do the kids really understand?" Leanna saw the pain in her big sister's eyes and detected the shakiness in her voice. "How does it effect them? Do the other parents understand?"

"We've had to explain that with everything being said about Keith, we can't risk other children being seen coming into our home. It's hardest for Emily. Her closest friends are from school and we don't know how much their parents understand. Matthew has a friend from church. His mother understands. She's one of the Child Care workers, and he's the only boy we let come over."

"We all know the hard times make us stronger," Leanna comforted, "but it's always harder when things hurt our loved ones."

"That's for sure," I agreed. "We'll just have to trust the Lord for understanding as well as strength and comfort. That's the principle we are putting into practice and it holds true for our children as well as for ourselves."

The night before Leanna left to return home to New Orleans she and Lynne both got to the heart of their concerns. "Lynne, I know this is so hard for you."

"Leanna, Keith is not guilty and he knows the Lord is able to see him through whatever. Our faith is being tested. We must believe the fact that God is not only in charge of keeping us strong, but he is in charge of the outcome."

"But I can't understand why this has happened. Keith is

such an unlikely person to be accused of these things,"
Leanna insisted.

"We don't know the purpose either," Lynne said. "It's
frustrating! Sometimes I cry, 'O.K., Lord, it's been long
enough—clue me in, what's going on, what's happening?'"
Lynne's fingers shook slightly as she twisted her napkin.

"I tell myself people sometimes suffer for things they don't
do. Good people get sick and die and some people go to jail
when they haven't committed a crime. Lynne, what will you
do if he isn't cleared?"

They both sat and cried for awhile.

Finally, Lynne said, "I know I could rely on my nursing.
I've been offered a full time position at the hospital, but I've
told them for now I want to keep things just as they are. The
decision is going to be, do we stay here or move closer to
where Keith might be taken? I don't have to make those
decisions yet.

"Leanna, it's hard, I walk into a room sometimes and cry
without warning. But you'll not find me hanging my head in
despair. I know I can't handle this but the Lord will handle
it for me." Lynne reached for her Bible, opening it to the same
verse she'd shared with Emily the night I was in jail nearly
three months before. ". . .We are afflicted in every way, but
not crushed, we're perplexed but not despairing, persecuted
but not forsaken, struck down but not destroyed."

"But this is so hideous," Leanna cried, slamming her fist
on the table.

"I know it's hideous. It's big time stuff and it's horrible to
go through. But I know we're not forsaken and we're not in
total despair. We won't be destroyed. I'm clinging to that
verse, Leanna. I force myself to focus on God and His
promises; it's become an hour by hour discipline."

After Leanna left we continued the tedious wait for the
preliminary hearing only to have Charlie call and tell us it
was postponed again. "The judge has rescheduled it for
September 28," he said.

On Friday, June 26, Lynne asked me, "Did you read the
paper yet today?" I'd just come home for lunch.

"No, why? Is there something I should see?"

"Well, I don't know just how it will affect us but DeVouton's
resigning from the St. Charles prosecutor's office for a higher
paying position in the St. Louis County office."

"Did it say who's taking his cases?" I reached for the paper lying on the end of the table.

"No, but you're listed with two murder cases as being the difficult cases which replacements will be handling. Hannah's hired another man, a Mr. Zimmerman, I think."

When Mr. Zimmerman was assigned as my prosecutor, my loyal friend, Andy Mueller gave me his opinion. "I feel sorry for him. He's a good attorney and he's been handed a hot potato. A hand grenade with no pin. He's told, 'Here, you convict this guy of child molestation' and what's he got, less than a month to prepare his case? And there ain't no case."

"Well, you and I know that, Andy, but the prosecutor still doesn't. Terry Gannon, the director from VOCAL, called the other day and according to a friend of her's who works in the St. Charles Division of Family Services' office, the prosecutor has a full time investigator on me. They think I'm involved in Satanic ritualistic abuse and they're trying to get information from California because they think there's a kind of network and all these cases across the country are related."

It's not often I loose sleep but my friend, Al Johnson, who preached periodically, began making occasional comments to members that concerned me. "It isn't that Al believes I've abused these boys," I told Lynne. "He thinks I need to be reaching out to the accusing families."

"But Keith, that's impossible. It isn't safe for one thing, with the hostility some of them have for you, besides Charlie feels they can too easily misunderstand something you might say and use it against you. Doesn't Al see that?"

"Apparently not. Al seems to have his mind pretty well set. He's asked if he could preach while we're on vacation. I'll probably let him."

In August we heard from Charlie that the prosecutor's office had scheduled the Child Care workers for depositions later in the month. Still, there seemed no reason why we shouldn't leave on vacation.

We had reservations at Windermere, the Missouri Baptist retreat center located on the Lake of the Ozarks in south central Missouri. As Matthew and I loaded our bags into the van, Lynne brought out a box of food. "I can hardly wait to get to Windermere," she said.

Heading west on I-70 I mentioned to Lynne, "The cassette on the dash is yesterday's service." We'd been out of town for the day and Al had preached. As Lynne slipped the cassette into the player, I glanced at the rear view mirror and noticed that the kids had already fallen asleep.

After the music portion of the service, Al began to speak. Although he said he loved me, he sliced me to shreds. He told the church our current problems with the Child Care were the result of sin in the pastor's life and God's blessing had left the church. Then he called everyone to repentance and prayer.

"Keith, what's happened to him? He's always been the peacemaker at church, always smoothing out misunderstandings."

I shook my head. "What's done is done. The people who know me will know that what he said isn't true. We just have to go on and trust God to see us through."

We spent our days swimming, fishing, and hiking with the kids and at night, when they were asleep, we wrestled with our hurt and anger. I asked God to show me if there was reason for Al's accusations, yet I never felt any conviction of guilt.

"Keith, it wouldn't hurt so if it wasn't coming from someone in our own church family," Lynne commented. "Doesn't he know you better than that?" We both felt betrayed. I poured my anger out to God. He took it and by the end of the week I could pray for Al with the right attitude again.

"The PA is filing motions saying the children are psychologically unavailable." Charlie's soothing voice had a calming effect even though his news was disturbing. "They are wanting to admit hearsay evidence."

"What about the videotaped interviews of the children, are they going to use them?" I asked.

"They say the videos are too long and there are only a few minutes when the children say anything. I'm going to subpoena the children, but I think they are being primed not to say anything.

"There are new rumors out now, too." Charlie continued. "They're saying you didn't take a child to your house, but to another person's house and the detectives are investigating that."

"I guess it keeps them in work, looking for something that doesn't exist."

"They are still into this devil worship thing because some child drew a picture of an eye in a triangle. By the way, did you pick up on the quote from Dr. Underwager in *The Child*

Abuse Industry?" Charlie had me wait while he looked it up and read.

"'There is a remarkable similarity in the images children produce under interrogation—whether or not they have been abused. You see the same progression. First, they speak of fondling, then penetration, then monsters, leading on to the killing of small animals and finally the ritualistic murder of babies and adults.'"[5]

Charlie abruptly changed the subject. "Mr. Whaley, the attorney appointed by the insurance company, wants to meet September 16 at my office. The police have released for our viewing prior to the preliminary hearing one video tape of Tim Raymond being interviewed by therapist Tish LaRock at Cardinal Glennon Hospital. Whaley wants to see that tape with us."

When we arrived Bill Seibel, Charlie's partner, joined us as we briefly reviewed the notes and statements of the parents and reports from Cardinal Glennon Hospital, then we looked at the video.

"I've interrogated a lot of children as prosecutor," Bill said, shaking his head and letting out a long sigh, "but I've never questioned them like this woman Tish LaRock. Who is she anyway?"

"She's the nurse practitioner at Cardinal Glennon Hospital who interviewed most of the boys in this case," Charlie answered.

The next day I met Andy Mueller at Mr. Steak for lunch. "Hey, Little Preacher, what's up?" he greeted.

"Well, Charlie Bridges and his associate Bill Seibel were at the church today trying to lift the cast iron manhole cover from the storm drain in the upper parking lot."

"Don't tell me, must be more rumors."

"Yep. One boy is now saying I put him down there."

"Well, that's good. How'd you get the manhole open?"

"He said I opened it with a knife."

Andy leaned back in the booth. "Let's see, now. I can just picture this. There's a manhole outside the church. I'm pretty strong but I think it's all I can do to get it open with a tire iron. So you did all of this holding a wiggling five year old, cause no kid in his right mind's gonna to be put down a dark hole." He shook his head. "And you did this with a buck knife?"

"I don't know what kind of a knife, they just said a knife."

"Preacher, if you can do that with a kid in one hand and a pocket knife in the other, get a cast iron manhole cover off, Man, you're somethin'." Andy stabbed his index finger at me. "And the next time my wife decides to change the living room furniture around you can do it, Pal, 'cause I ain't gonna lift it again."

Lynne's brother Pat came from Texas on Sunday to be with us for the preliminary hearing.

At nine the next morning, September 28, unsure of what to expect, Lynne, Pat, and I walked into the courtroom for the preliminary hearing that would determine if the charges against me would be bound over for trial. Charlie was there to represent me, with Bill Seibel as his assistant. John Zimmerman, as expected, was the prosecutor.

It was the same small courtroom I'd been in for the arraignment. When we recessed for the first morning break I walked down a narrow hallway to the men's restroom. As I neared the door, the grandfather of one of the children came out with a fist up. If it wasn't for a quick-moving deputy, I'd have been flattened.

When the court was dismissed for the second break I was relieved to see Andy a few feet away making a silly face at me. I motioned him over.

"I need to go to the restroom, Andy, come with me."

"O.K., let's go." A teasing smile curled his lips, "Am I the potty security guard?" he whispered.

"Exactly," I confirmed and related the earlier incident. From then on Andy made himself my personal body guard. Throughout the entire first day I sat mesmerized as I listened to the professionals reveal their accumulated evidence.

"I'm going to object to this as being hearsay," Charlie interrupted. "... It violates the defendant's rights of confrontation for [this witness] to tell this Court what the parents have told her." He explained to me earlier that a new law allowed for hearsay testimony of children, but this was third party hearsay.

"Overruled," Judge William Lohmar dictated. Charlie asked that his objection be recorded and made continuous throughout the hearing.

Detective Harvey testified that the police in one county couldn't locate a church I'd previously served. I knew that couldn't be true, because former members in both Carrollton and Columbia, Missouri had let us know that police in their area had interviewed them.

Altogether, three policemen and four therapists testified for the prosecution. These witnesses kept inserting "behavioral indicators" among reported allegations from the boys.

Dr. Judy Tindall, a licensed psychologist, who had counselled two of the boys, took the stand. "Children often display a kind of disempowerment," she said. "They don't feel like they can take charge of their life. . . ." As three other therapists recited their evidence and children's histories, we heard the familiar theme, "Children don't lie about these things."

Zimmerman called Dr. James Monteleone, the State's unchallenged expert. His balding head, neck, and shoulders seemed to melt into his pear-shaped body as he approached the witness stand. I was surprised that he had no notes as the prosecutor led him through the names and medical findings of the seven boys.

". . . I examined six of the seven [boys] and Dr. Dearhoff examined Alex Jackson. I read [Dr. Dearhoff's] notes, and there were no physical findings on him."

"Why don't we start with Chad Walker?" Zimmerman requested.

". . . I found his anal sphincter had some elasticity and it dilated easily and there was a small tag inside the anus about six o'clock." Dr. Monteleone described a tag as a piece of tissue torn loose, then declared, "His [Chad Walker's] physical findings were consistent with sexual abuse."

"With regard to Paul Stevens. . . .?"

". . . Two small scars and a dimple. No tag. . . . Where there was old trauma you get . . . a dimple. . . . It does not negate sexual abuse."

"Move to Todd Brady."

". . . Physical findings are not remarkable, but this does not negate sexual abuse."

". . . Is it possible to determine that a child has not been sexually abused simply by a physical exam?" Zimmerman asked.

"No, it isn't possible. I can never say a child was not sexually abused. Never." Dr. Monteleone's confidence was smugly adamant, and I wondered what purpose the Sexual Abuse Management unit served other than to validate a therapist's opinion.

Lynne blinked in amazement too, at the doctor's statement and wrote in her notes,"What kind of medical opinion is that? His statements sounded like double talk—if he can never say 'never,' it's pointless to send a child there."

"Validate," we later discovered, means simply to stamp a report as official. Legally, the validator is saying of an investigator, "I won't stick my neck out by saying a child is not abused."

"Move to Mark Herns."

"I think this is the one that was the most dramatic of all. . . . Very upset and apprehensive . . . a behavioral indicator. . . . The anus was markedly dilated. Some funneling. But no tears or tagging. . . . You can see almost like a funnel through the anus, and this child had that."

"Would it be fair to say with regard to Mark Herns that a physical exam would be consistent with sexual abuse and on top of that the physical exam would be consistent with repeated sexual abuse?"

"Yes."

"Move to Tim Raymond."

". . . The child demonstrated a number of behavioral indicators. Typical findings consistent with sexual abuse as stated by child."

"O.K. And the last child I want to ask you about is Curtis Farrow."

". . .Alert, very cooperative. [With the] anus, there was some fecal soiling. Otherwise, not remarkable. Although physical findings are not remarkable this does not negate sexual abuse. . . . Fecal soiling can be an indicator too."

I recognized Chad Walker's mother as soon as Zimmerman called her to the stand. From her testimony I realized her son, Chad, must have been one of the boys interviewed by detectives Harvey and Pope before they interrogated me at the police station. Chad was the one who had allegedly identified me at the gas station and claimed I put vegetables in his bottom. According to the police, he had been the one to first name me as the "bad man." Mrs. Walker added more sordid details.

"When they were taken to a house they were made to do more of the sexual acts, . . .there were pictures of him and other kids on the walls . . . without their clothes on. . . . There were some pretty girls there . . . making a movie and they had him take his clothes off and had him kiss the pretty girls' big boobies."

I was a father who had avoided changing my own babies' diapers whenever possible. I couldn't begin to think up these things I was being accused of. As their claims become more exaggerated I found I was emotionally disengaging myself from the person they were accusing,

On cross-exam Charlie asked Mrs. Walker, "Prior to Linda Cooper [from DFS] coming out and talking to him, he had no nightmares?"

"Not prior to that, he had not."

"When Linda Cooper was over on November 20, 1986, did your son mention Brother Keith to you. . ."

"He did not."

"You indicate in your notes dated January 5, '87 and January 11, '87, that your son told you Brother Keith had a boy by the name of Joey and a girl by the name of Cissy?"

"That's correct." Now the anonymous phone call we received in January about Joey and Cissy being our downfall made sense.

Mr. and Mrs. Roger Jackson testified. I was anxious to hear them because their son—not interviewed by the police until February 24—was the one the police claimed broke the case. Both stated on the witness stand at my preliminary hearing that their son had said I "peed" on his chest and in his mouth, put him in a trash can, touched his "dee dee," and put my "dee dee" in his pants, and a rock in his rectum. We later learned from subpoenaed notes of the Jacksons and their son's therapist that during the several weeks it took for Alex to reveal his "secrets," his behavior became more aggressive and unmanageable and his sleep more disturbed.

In her testimony at the preliminary hearing, Mrs. Jackson referred to her notes and reported Alex as saying, "Brother Keith peed in my [Alex's] mouth and it wasn't like normal pee."

". . . Did you disclose this to the police?"

"Yes. . . . We were asked to keep most things Alex related to us and write them down."

"What kind of instructions did you get from the police," Zimmerman asked, "or from any other person regarding how to question Alex, or whether you should question him, or the method of questioning. . . .?"

"We were [to] let him talk as he wanted to. . . . Other times I was instructed by Kathleen Williams, [the counselor recommended to us] to help Alex go through the process and try to talk about it, but Alex . . . . was reluctant to talk."

"'. . . I was supposed to die but I just went to sleep,'" Mrs. Jackson read from her notes. She claimed that Alex said I took him to my house and photographed him undressed, put needles in his stomach and legs, and poured blood on him and his friend, Paul. Mrs. Jackson further reported that Alex told her while he was still in the Child Care that I pulled his hair and hit his face and back.

Charlie's cross examination helped me breathe easier. Mrs. Jackson recalled when Detective Pope asked Alex if he had seen me pee on him. She also recalled other important information when Charlie asked, "How many times prior to February 24, 1987 did Alex deny that he had been sexually abused?"

"At least three or four times. My husband asked him the questions and just asked him if. . . . he was ever forced to touch Brother Keith's private parts and he said no."

Charlie continued questioning. "Do you remember Detective Pope asking Alex if there was a devil's pit?"

"Yes." She said yes again when Charlie asked if the first time Alex said I was the bad guy was after Detective Pope talked to him.

Four-year-old Paul Steven's mother admitted under oath that she had asked her son leading questions. She also conceded that Paul didn't begin showing signs of fear until after he started talking about what supposedly happened.

Mr. and Mrs. James Farrow's testimonies were much like the Jacksons and Mrs. Stevens. According to the Farrows, their son Curtis claimed he'd been taken various places and stuck with pins. The Farrows said Curtis was hesitant at first to talk about what had happened because he'd been threatened if he "tells" things.

When Charlie cross-examined the Farrows, they testified that Curtis suddenly began hating women during the time he was being questioned by a therapist.

He'd had an obsession to tie his mother up with anything he could find whenever she sat or lay down. "When he was forbidden to tie her up," Mr. Farrow said, "we'd find him with the doors locked in his bedroom, and he'd have himself tied up and gagged."

Other than the word of the parents and opinion of the professionals, the prosecution had no hard evidence of my involvement in any alleged molestation. However, the prosecution did not realize they had real problems until after Charlie's cross examination of prosecution witnesses and testimony by the church Child Care workers. Problems that couldn't be ignored when everyone returned two weeks later for the conclusion of the hearing to view Charlie's videotaped depositions of three boys.

Only a few spectators showed up for the last day of the hearing but Andy was among them, and we stood chatting just before the judge called the court to order. "I expected to see [Chief Prosecutor] Hannah here for at least part of this hearing," Andy commented as he looked around. "Why the no show?"

"I understand he's in Australia right now." The judge was just entering from his chambers.

"Learning to run a kangaroo court, I bet," Andy cracked and headed for his seat.

Charlie made only a few brief comments before we viewed his deposition interviews of the three boys. The three children positively identified former prosecuting attorney John DeVouton as sexually abusing them. Even more shocking for the prosecution, one boy identified Police Chief Patrick McCarrick's home while another identified Detective Pope's home as locations where abuse took place. When Zimmerman cross-examined, two of the boys refused to recant their testimonies.

The room was still buzzing with muffled whispers when one child identified a Missouri Supreme Court judge and a doctor on the Missouri Arts Council as the man and woman the boy and two of his friends "killed" while with "Brother Keith."

The newspaper headline read, "Boys' Testimony Called 'Fiction'." "Obviously, children can make up stories," Zimmerman was quoted as saying. Police Chief McCarrick called the stories "a lot of baloney."

Andy Mueller showed wry amusement when I showed him the report in the newspaper. "Seems McCarrick was one of the detectives quoting the professionals a few months ago, claiming 'children don't lie about these things," Andy said, shaking his head. "He sort'uv changed his tune now that his name's mentioned."

Nevertheless, Judge Lohmar ruled that he had found enough evidence for my case to be tried by a jury on 15 felony accounts of sexual child abuse of seven young boys.

Chapter Eight

The Alliance of the "Professionals"

"... The law, intentionally or not, gives full immunity to all agents of the state. . ."

"You know, Reverend, when I came into this case," Bill Seibel explained to me shortly after the preliminary hearing, "I truly believed there was a real possibility you were guilty."

"What convinced you otherwise?" I asked. I liked Bill's straightforward honesty.

"The evidence tells me you didn't do anything." Bill gave me a long steady look. I felt his sincerity. "Really, it's a process of going through the evidence. I got the impression from the prosecutor's office that your church's Child Care workers were a coven of witches torturing these children. When I met with them I saw little old ladies who looked like grandmothers. You might as well tell me that June Cleaver, Beaver's mother is a witch too." Bill stretched back into his executive chair and talked easily.

"I took notes from the video of your police interrogation which we subpoened. I heard you say approximately 75 times, 'I didn't do anything.' It was an intense interrogation, nearly two hours long, and you never wavered. Guilty people admit to something, usually a minor version of the charge against them.

"Sexual abuse is one of the easiest cases to allege," he explained. "And what's more, no judge is going to risk his political career by making an independent decision to throw a case out. He'll bring it to court and let the jury make the decision."

My feelings soared when Bill said he was convinced of my innocence, then plummeted when he mentioned how judges felt about sexual child abuse cases. Almost daily Lynne and I experienced emotional roller coaster rides like this.

It was now a year since the nightmare began. "Have yourself a merry little Christmas. . . ." Perry Como's mellow voice carried above the din of Christmas shoppers, but failed to drown out the one unasked question that sulked in the shadows of my mind: Will I be with my family in 1988?

I wandered in a daze with Lynne from one store to another unable to decide on gifts for Lynne and Emily and Matthew. I wanted this Christmas to be special and I purchased each gift with a pang of uncertainty—or was it finality?

Lynne's voice startled me as we neared the men's wear department in Sears. "Keith, you really do need another sports coat," she insisted.

"I can wait. I'd rather give the kids a nice Christmas." To myself I thought, Will I be where I can wear it? There was also the carpet in the kitchen worn to the rubber, and the water stain in the ceiling of Emily's bedroom. Not to mention the mounting legal fees.

We had only Christmas day to spend in DeSoto with my family and we wanted to leave our troubles in St. Charles. My brother, Bob, and his wife Carolyn were there. Dad had recovered from his pneumonia of the past spring and was generally cheerful, but as Mother and I were talking, she fell into tears. "Keith, one of my best friends said, 'Maybe it's God's will for you to go to prison.' Oh, Son, how could that be?"

"No, Mother, I'm sure what she's trying to say is that God can use the bad things in our lives and bring good from them. Remember Joseph in the Bible, when he said of his brothers, 'they meant it for evil, but God meant it for good?.'"

Dad had something to say. "Ran into our local chief of police awhile back, Son. He apologized for the department having to arrest you."

Mother dried her tears and a lighter time prevailed. When Mother served the chocolate cake, Carolyn quipped, "Keith, I'll send you a chocolate cake with a file in it if you go to prison."

Jim and Laura Rogers and Terry Gannon continued to supply us with articles and information from seminars they attended. One day a friendly voice on the phone introduced herself as Carol Marks, a licensed counselor from California. "I'm visiting my mother in St. Louis," she said, "and just read an article about your case in the newspaper. I counsel people who are falsely accused of child abuse. From all I can understand, you fall into that category. I'm going to send you some information which might help in your defense." I thanked her and hung up, not realizing how helpful her materials would be in the future.

Now that the preliminary hearing was over Charlie and Bill could get copies of all the depositions, written reports and notes of the parents, therapists, and the Sexual Abuse Management unit at Cardinal Glennon Hospital, plus the revealing videotaped police interviews of the boys. Charlie handed me a stack of videos. "Get these typed up word for word and describe any clear body language." It would take weeks for Lynne and me, along with a couple of volunteers, to accomplish the mountainous job.

Charlie was also digging in a nearby medical school library, researching physical findings in case histories of child abuse and comparing these with other information available on my case. Going far beyond the call of duty, Charlie literally lived my case day and night, while Bill Seibel relieved him by handling much of the routine in their law office.

I stopped by the law office nearly every week and we shared findings back and forth. One afternoon Charlie shoved a large book across his desk to me. "This is the most exhaustive study of accusations of child sexual abuse I've found." He pointed to a highlighted passage. I read aloud from Hollida Wakefield and Dr. Ralph Underwager's book, *Accusations of Child Sexual Abuse.*

"'Prior to the first official contact, the parents, if they suspect abuse, . . .will question the child. . . . Retrospective descriptions of this first interrogation begins when the investigation official first talks to the reporting adult and gets the information that led to the report. If the investigating official has the bias that children must always be believed and that all accusations are true, the initial contact with the child will be based upon the prior assumption that alleged abuse really happened. This bias markedly affects the outcome of the investigation.'[6]

"Well Charlie, it will be interesting to see if this is true in my case."

When we studied the writen notes and reports it became evident that Keri Walker, the mother of little Chad, had been unable to accept the conclusion of the DFS that the soap incident could not be substantiated. By referral of Cardinal

Glennon Hospital, she had taken her son in November, 1986
to Ms. Holly Carson, a professional counselor with the Grey
Psychological Clinic. This was almost a month before the
first allegations were made against me.

Charlie pulled a copy of some of Ms. Carson's subpoenaed
notes from a pile on his desk. "According to these, Chad did
not verbally give any information to Ms. Carson that indicated sexual abuse. It was his non-verbal behavior and other
behavioral changes as reported by the parents that apparently made Ms. Carson think he could have been a victim
of abuse."

Charlie continued, "Then, on her own, Mrs. Walker consulted with Dr. Juli Antanow, a pediatrician. Dr. Antanow
states in her evaluation that Chad liked the Child Care and
that she found in Chad no evidence of physical abuse. Also,
she later advised Mr. Walker not to pressure the child for
information.

"Here's something else. The records show that Mrs.
Walker took Chad to four different pediatricians during a
three month period."

Charlie picked up another document. "In early December,
1986 Mrs. Walker contacted the Farrows and told them
about her son's behavior. Within the week, by her own
admission, four other families had come forward with
suspicions that something had happened to their sons at
your Child Care Center."

When I shared some of this information with the Rogers',
Jim noted, "Other complaints of child abuse would not be
difficult for someone to make. The law allows for anonymous
reports through the hot line to the Division of Family Services. Laura and I visited 17 DFS offices in nearby counties.
A number of DFS people told us that they call the child abuse
hot line themselves if they don't get evidence on one visit and
want to get back into a home for more investigation."

"Why can't we investigate the families who have made
these allegations against me?" I asked Charlie. "The police
have limited their entire investigation to me. Not one other
person has been considered, much less investigated?"

"The police are noted for tunnel vision, and that's not
necessarily bad," Charlie said. "Even so, if we did investigate
the families and found something suspicious," Charlie wisely
reasoned, "the court would probably not let the information
about the families in as evidence because they are not the

ones on trial. We have to concentrate on building your defense, not establishing a case against them. I have discovered something interesting though. According to notes from a therapist, one of the parents suffered sexual abuse as a child."

"That goes along with something I found. Let me read it," I replied, as I shuffled through some papers.

"'. . .Adults may be hypersensitive to signs of abuse—for example, parents who were themselves abused, social workers, teachers, and doctors who are under threat of criminal penalties to report suspected abuse. . . . In these cases, clumsy, suggestive, or abusive questioning can lead children to say, and even believe, things that did not happen in the way suggested.'"[7]

As we reviewed the videos from police, therapists, and hospital counselors, this opinion was confirmed.

"Before you leave I want to tell you," Charlie said, "that I asked Dr. Coleman, the psychiatrist, for names of some medical practitioners who might testify for us. He recommended Dr. David Paul from Guy's Hospital in London and Dr. Robert W. ten Bensel from the Mayo Clinic in Minnesota. Dr. ten Bensel is also Professor of Public Health and Pediatrics at the University of Minnesota."

Charlie picked up a heavy transcript that looked an inch thick. "Here's the take-home work which you've been waiting for—the complete transcript of the preliminary hearing."

"Thanks Charlie, it'll make good bedtime stories."

Later that evening after the children were in bed, Lynne and I brought a stack of videos, the preliminary hearing transcript, notes, and an assortment of journal articles to the living room. I read some excerpts from the transcript to Lynne.

Listen to what the prosecution lawyer [John Zimmerman] asked Officer Muschler. "'Do you have any specialized training or have you attended seminars with regard to interviewing young children in a situation like this?' 'No,' Muschler replied."

"Let's see for ourselves," Lynne said, plopping down in front of our TV with a yellow legal pad and pen. As she picked up the video of the police interrogations of the boys taken December 10, earlier in the day before detectives Pope and Harvey first questioned me, she added, "And while we're at it I might just as well start transcribing." When she started the video we learned that Patrolman Muschler drove Chad to the police station by way of McDonald's. His mother and Detective Pope joined them at the police station for the interview and after a few warm up questions Muschler asked.

"Who are we going to take care of?"

"Oh, the bad guys," Chad replied.

"Bad guy?" Muschler corrected.

Detective Pope decided to pry. "Do you know your friends?" Chad shook his head and appeared totally bored. "Do you have any friends at all." Chad still didn't respond. "O.K., who's this bad guy you talked to Officer Muschler about."

"It's a bad guy."

"He's a bad guy," Pope corrected again. "What's his name?" Chad didn't have an answer and just sat. "It's O.K., you can tell me, it's O.K.," Pope assured. Chad put his hand on his forehead as if in deep thought.

"Chad, what was that bad guy's name? Remember?" Muschler coaxed, "Oh, what was his name? Yeah, you remember, don't you? What did we call him?"

"Uhhhh." Chad acted as if he didn't know what to say.

"What did you tell me his name was?" Muschler's voice carried a slight edge.

"Uhhhh, I don't remember his name again." The impatience in Chad's voice matched Muschler's.

"Yes, you do." Muschler chided. Then he talked about Chad's friends. Soon he asked, "What did Todd call the bad man?"

"I don't remember it," Chad answered disgustedly.

"Oh, come on, you told me, remember?" Muschler's voice softened and both he and Detective Pope asked more general questions about the school and activities. When Chad seemed less irritated, Pope asked, "Did you ever leave that room?"

"No."

"Chad, remember what I told you?" Pope scolded. "That we always have to tell the truth because we're all friends and you want to be a policeman? Will you tell me what you were talking about with Officer Muschler here? Will you tell me about that?"

"About bad guys?" Chad mumbled, then leaned over to his mother. "What was his name?" he whispered loudly.

"I don't remember either, you'll have to tell them, but it's

O.K. if you tell it," she said.

"It's good," Pope agreed. Chad ignored Pope's prompting and whispered to his mother again.

"I don't know his name either," he whispered

The police gave up on a name for awhile and tried for a description.

"What does this bad guy look like?" Pope asked.

"He looks like mean."

"What color is his skin?"

"He's a black man."

"He's a black man?" Pope was not satisfied. "You know what black is, don't you? See Mama's [black] purse over there . . . ?Does he look like that? Is he that color?"

"He's a boy, black," Chad mumbled.

"Chad!" Muschler barked. "Remember what we were talking about? Do you remember what you told me he looked like? Remember that?" Chad finally agreed the man had skin like his mama's, then Muschler asked, "Does he have anything on his face?"

"No."

"Does he ever wear anything on his face?"

"No."*

"What was his name? You remember, don't you? You just don't want to tell us," Muschler chided.

"Nope, I don't remember, uh, remember." Chad appeared bored with the whole business.

Pope tried again. "O.K., tell me about this bad man. What kind of bad things does the bad man do?"

"He hits people all the time." Chad slapped his own cheek several times.

"On your cheek? Does he ever hit any of your friends?" Muschler asked. Without waiting for a reply Pope cut in with his own suggestions.

"Did he hit you anywhere beside the cheek? The cheek on your face? Would he hit you anywhere else?"

"No."

"CHAD!" Muschler barked. "Remember, I'm here to protect you and nothing is going to happen to you."

"I know!" Chad yelled back, disgusted.

---

*   "I always wear glasses."

"Wait just a minute," Lynne jabbed the pause button and her eyes flashed anger. "Those two detectives have rejected every answer Chad has given them and now they're interpreting his actions. Keith, the boy didn't say anything about you hitting him." Without another word she started the video again.

Detective Muschler backed off for several minutes then attempted to extract a name with the use of anatomically correct child and adult male dolls.

I touched the pause button and reached for a copy of an article on the use of such dolls from *Phi Delta Kappan* magazine. I read some excerpts to Lynne.

"'Officials who investigate cases of suspected child abuse often have limited knowledge of children. Moreover, the procedures these officials use frequently lack reliability or validity.'

"'The use of anatomically correct dolls to investigate cases involving the sexual abuse of children is a case in point. No study has ever demonstrated that such dolls produce reliable and valid evidence.'"[8]

"Here's a clinical psychologist who totally agrees." Lynne passed to me the copy of a letter which was circulating around the VOCAL network. "This guy says that investigators using these dolls found that both abused and non-abused children handled them in the same way. And that children who had not been abused demonstrated hitting, cutting, tearing, and various sex acts with the same frequency as those who had been abused. These non-abused children with only the slightest amount of leading, could be easily led to indicate things to an adult that would appear to be abuse.[9] That's the findings of this man and other clinical psychologists, Keith. Don't our local therapists and investigators ever consider stuff like this?"

I shrugged. "Apparently not."

I hit the VCR play button again. The continuation of the police interview of Chad proved to be a classic example of what Lynne had learned from the psychologist.

As Chad played with the dolls, the police prompted him to pretend he was the boy doll and the bad man the man doll. Chad was instructed to show what the bad man did to him. As he bounced, banged, and tossed the dolls in a manner typical of a four year old boy, Muschler pelted him with questions: "Did he do more than that? . . . Did he hit you? He shook you? Did he ever do anything to you besides doing that. . . ?"

"No," Chad insisted.

"Chad!" Muschler's voice was stern. "Remember what we—what you told me," he corrected himself."

"I KNOW!" Chad returned the rebuff. After several minutes of hounding Chad, the police begin undressing the dolls and asked Chad to name the body parts. Pope was asking the questions.

"And what's this below the belly button?"

"Huh? What's this?" Chad looked puzzled and pointed to the penis surrounded by pubic hair. "I don't know, what is that?"

"Did you ever see that on the bad man?" Chad shook his head. "You never saw that on the bad man?" Uncomfortable innocence was the only way to describe Chad's expression as he continued to shake his head.

There were more questions about private parts. Then Muschler directed Chad's attention to his uneaten french fries and handing Chad one, asked, ". . . What do you want to say this stuff is?" Muschler handed Chad a french fry. ". . . . Show me what happened to your private part, using that [french fry]."

"I need two." Chad got another then went to the little boy doll.

"That's good, show me what happened. It's O.K.," Muschler coached.

"I KNOW!" Chad shouted and flipped the doll over on it's back.

"O.K., there's the private part," Muschler directed.

"Turn it over," Chad commanded as he stuck french fries in the penis.

"Yeah, what is that? What are we pretending that stuff is?" Muschler repeated, "Is that—what is it?"

"I'm calling these french fries."

"Yeah, but what are we pretending they are?" Pope interrupted.

"I pretend that these are food," Chad said, and he started sticking french fries into the boy doll's bottom.

"These are food," Muschler agreed. "Oh, is that what happened to the food? . . . Who showed you to put that there? Chad, did somebody show you to put that there?"

"Yes."

"Who?" Both men instantly asked in unison.

"Mommy!" Chad growled loudly.

"Who?" Muschler asked, surprised by the unexpected answer.

"Mommy."

"No, Mommy didn't show you," Muschler corrected. "I think somebody else showed you. . . . Who put that food back there? Who put that food in there?" Then showing Chad the bad man doll, he asked, "Who's this guy?"

"Bad guy," was Chad's only comment. The french fries had broken the monotony for Chad and he entertained himself by throwing them at the dolls. Everything he did elicited questions like, "How were you sitting? So what else did he do? Would he throw things at you?" Then Muschler tried again for a name.

"He used to come down and eat lunch with you. Who was the guy, remember. . . ? You just tell me where he took you. . . . ?"

"For a piggyback ride."

"Where?"

"For a piggyback ride."

"For a bike ride?"

"Nooooo."

After some 45 minutes of questioning and still no name given for the "bad guy," the sound of the tape mysteriously went off for 45-50 seconds. Officer Muschler was shown shaking Chad's hand just prior to the sound returning. Then the sound came on and from this point forward the police referred to the man doll as "Brother Keith."

"So Brother Keith was at the church?" Pope asked.

Muschler reached for the bad doll and handcuffed it. ". . . .We gotta put our handcuffs on Brother Keith, don't we. 'Cause he's bad."

From then on the police referred to the "bad man" doll as Brother Keith. Other food—peas, beans, corn, Danish [sweet rolls]—was mentioned and assumptions made by the police that the food was used in sex acts.

Later Detective Pope reached over and flattened the boy doll's penis. "Would Brother Keith take his hand and touch your 'willie' like that? . . . You can tell me if he did."

"It's O.K. because we're friends," Muschler prompted.

"He didn't," Chad denied, and kept shaking his head through more assumptive questioning.

After viewing more police interviews of the boys over a period of several nights, we realized that Chad's hour-and-twenty-minute interrogation was a carbon copy of the police interviews of all the boys. The intimidating and leading questions coupled with praise for the "right" answers and disapproval for the "wrong" responses armed the police with the testimony they sought.

"I guess we finally know where the allegations came from that led to your interrogation," Lynne commented when we finished transcribing the last police video. "I never would have believed police to use such psychological pressure on children."

"I know." I opened the preliminary hearing transcript again and started skimming the rest of Patrolman Muschler's testimony. "Get this, Lynne."

"Chad has said the bad man put donuts, corn, string beans in his private parts. Then Mr. Zimmerman asked Muschler, 'Did you at any time suggest what sort of things were placed there or where they were placed?' Muschler answered, 'No, he came up with them.'"

I continued reading from the transcript.

"Alright, now here's what Pope testified when Mr. Zimmerman asked him, 'At anytime did you suggest any answers to Chad during this interview on the basis of what you heard Vic Muschler say?' Detective Pope answered, 'No, sir.' Zimmerman asked, 'At any time did you lead the child at all? . . . . Did you at any time hear Officer Muschler lead the child or suggest any answers to the child?' 'No sir,' Pope denied.

"Then Mr. Zimmerman asked, 'Did you observe anything that was unusual with respect to his habits about food?' Pope replied, 'He used some of the food in a demonstration as to what had occurred to him. . . . Chad said that he needed something, and Officer Muschler said, 'Well, you can use these,' and he gave him some french fries."

After we completely finished going through the transcript I asked Lynne, "Did you notice that Chad said my name only once when he was asked to identify the bad doll?"

"Yes, I did, but even then he didn't say it until after Muschler repeatedly called the bad doll, 'Brother Keith.'"

"Now I understand, Lynne, why Charlie wanted the police interrogation transcribed verbatim. When I brought the first transcription to him, he read to me this paragraph from the book, *Accusations of Child Sexual Abuse;*

"'Frequently, interviewers introduce a statement, a topic, a question, to which the child either gives no response, a denial, or a minimal response. After repeated questioning, the child may nod or answer yes. But in the report of the interview, the interviewer claims that the child said the statement... Denials which may have preceded the eventual affirmation are seldom mentioned.'[10]

"By the way, Charlie mentioned that he counted as many as 75 denials from one child before that child made any allegations against me."

Nearly every evening Lynne and I transcribed more from the police tapes and other subpoenaed material. We'd play a few words, hit the pause button, write what we heard, rewind it to double check, then continue to inch our way forward sentence by sentence through each tape.

Frequently we stopped to talk about what was on a tape. "I can't comprehend Detective Pope's reasoning, Lynne. Here's his explanation about why he didn't videotape the testimony the police claimed 'broke' my case. I went back and read from the preliminary hearing transcript, beginning with a question by Charlie to Pope.

"'... You asked some leading questions, you got some corroboration; is that right?'

"'I interviewed Alex as a witness, not as a victim.'

"'And you wouldn't consider that a victim if Alex and Tim and Paul were present when a man pees on them? You don't think that's a victim of sexual abuse?'

"'I think he was a witness.'"

"'A man exposed himself and pees on a child and you think that's a witness as opposed to a victim?'

"'I took it as a witness.'"

Lynne took the transcript from me. "Keith, I forgot something. Pope admitted on cross-exam that the police never investigated the story that says you put a boy down a manhole. They didn't record or investigate any allegations of devil worship, nor did they canvass our neighborhood to find witnesses of our activities at home."

One day after lunch, I visited with Jim and Laura Rogers. "Isn't there any way to stop the apparent lying on the witness stand?" I asked.

"No, there isn't," Jim answered.

Laura pulled a video from their files of a lawyer from the Missouri Attorney General's Office. "He was speaking at the

1987 Child Abuse Training Conference to state approved professionals," she explained.

I could hardly believe my ears when I heard this man say, "You as a witness have an absolute privilege, even if you lie."

"But what about their oath?" Lynne cried, when I told her about it. "They swear to tell the truth, the whole truth."

"As horrendous as it is, Dear, the law, intentionally or not, gives full legal immunity to all agents of the state which includes doctors, educators, social workers, and other agents of the state. Only a few legislators are starting to admit this was not the original intent of the law." Frustrated, we dropped the subject and went back to transcribing.

It wasn't long before Lynne spoke up. "I've been reading through Dr. Judy Tindall's preliminary hearing notes, Keith. She was the licensed psychologist who saw little Paul eight times and Tim Raymond once. She records Paul suffering some of the symptoms of sexual abuse—fears of going to the basement, going outside, and many dreams. Keith, that doesn't necessarily mean a thing." Lynne pulled her reading glasses off when she looked up at me. "In all my childhood development classes the instructors emphasized that fears and dreams are normal for children and nearly every parenting magazine on the market today reinforces that belief.

"Keith, I've been looking over Kathleen William's interviews—remember she's the one who saw Alex 17 times. It's interesting that his behavior and allegations became more bizarre throughout therapy.

"If Alex's behavior was getting as bad as Williams indicated, I'm surprised she didn't refer him to a psychiatrist," Lynne concluded. "After all, her Masters is in Social Work, she's not even a licensed psychologist." I thumbed through the transcript of the preliminary hearing to find her testimony. I read it to Lynne, starting with a question from Charlie.

"'Did you believe everything that Alex told you?'

"'Did I believe everything? Yes.'

"'Did Alex ever tell you that he was in a room, there was fire and smoke and snakes and bears, and blood was put on him?'"

"'Yes.'

"'And you believed that?'

"'I believe that's what he experienced, yes. . . . I believe the essence of what he tells me.'

"Lynne, I can still see the expression on Bill Seibel's face when she said that on the stand. He leaned over toward me and said, 'That little boy was describing a scene from 'Indiana Jones and The Temple of Doom?'"

"Bill's right," Lynne said as she started going through the stack of articles again. "Listen to this, 'Children . . . do not remember the origins of their knowledge, and they often mistake memories of dreams for memories of actual events.'[11] "Huh," Lynne snickered, "Art Linkletter said it best, remember? 'Kids say the darndest things.'"

On another evening, I was looking at preliminary hearing testimony by the therapist Shirley Williams when Lynne arrived home after work. She curled up on the couch beside me and began reading aloud what I'd highlighted.

"'The most telling behavior with regard to Mark H. was [that] he told me that Brother Keith had a T shirt . . . that he wore that had a lion, and Mark said that Brother Keith told him if he would tell a secret the lion would come to life and eat him up. After more sessions [Mark and I] were talking about 'The Wizard of Oz', and I unfortunately said 'the lion.' . . . His entire behavior changed to[ward] me.'

"'[Mark] asked me to draw a lion [and] he would put a penis on the lion. At that point Mark got up and got on my lap and dropped his pants . . . because I wasn't drawing it accurately. And that probably was the most telling behavior of Mark.'

"Keith, Mark never verbalized any specific instances of sexual abuse to Ms. Williams."

"That's right, he sure didn't. And remember that Shirley Williams holds a Masters in Clinical Child Psychology, but she too was an unlicensed counselor. Shirley Williams received referrals from Cardinal Glennon Hospital. She referred one boy to Kathleen Williams."

I flipped several pages through the transcript. "Remember this, Lynne? Charlie is still questioning Shirley Williams. Charlie asked her, 'Have you had an opportunity to talk to these children about the possibility of their coming to testify in this proceeding?'

"Shirley answered, '. . .I did with Chad Walker. . . . I [gave] him a magic rock to carry.'

"Charlie wanted to know what she meant by a 'magic rock.'

"'To empower him,' she said. She found a rock in a cave that had a spring running through it. 'So I told [Chad],' she said, 'that the rock was magic and it was powerful and it would help him to have the courage to come here [to testify]."'

I skimmed several more pages while Lynne got ready for bed. Lynne came back and I read aloud more of the exchange between Charlie and Shirley Williams, starting with a statement by Ms. Williams.

"'Children deal very heavily in metaphor.'

"'When you say metaphor, isn't that also otherwise known as fantasy?'

"'I call it metaphor. . . . Where it appears that I'm losing track of reality the child will bring me back to reality and say, 'That's just pretend.'

"'So when you told Chad Walker about the magic rock and he could take that into court with him and that would make him powerful, did he bring you back to reality?'

"'Not at that point in time. . .'

"'Part of your therapy is, in fact, to deal in fantasy is it not?'

"'To empower children.'

"'In dealing in this fantasy you then interpret the meanings of their statements; is that correct?'

"'Occasionally.'"

"Keith," Lynne interjected, "didn't Dr. Coleman have something to say about pretend methods of questioning?"

"Yes, I think he did," I said and reached for the dogeared stack of photographed articles. When I found it I started reading. "'. . .Children use dolls, puppets, or drawings to make up stories—not to stick to the facts. . . . Even worse is the result when the adult interviewer is already convinced that sexual abuse has taken place and (perhaps unwittingly) uses play methods to coax some evidence from the child.'"[12]

We each picked up the manuscripts we held and studied silently until something else caught my attention.

"Look here, Lynne." I came to Shirley Williams testimony about ritualism. "Charlie has just handed her Exhibits L and K. Now he asked her, 'And what to you is the significance of the star, the circle around the triangle with a small circle?'

"'It started becoming apparent that there may have been some ritualistic behaviors occurring with the children, and those are some of the symbols of the ritualism.'

"'And you drew these?'

"'Yes. They were trying to describe some things but it's very difficult for children to be concrete.'

"'When they couldn't be concrete you decided you would draw a star with a circle in it and a triangle in it?'

"Therapeutically you assume it has, indeed, happened to the children. . . .'"

"Therapeutically nothing!" Lynne exploded. "She built her own case on nothing but assumption."

"Let me read on. Charlie asked about her file on Mark Herns. Charlie then read from the file her note to Mark's parents. 'Buy him a toy tiger and let him do whatever he wants with it. Help him kill it, find out how Brother Keith would change, counteract that with your own magic.'

"'You told the parents to take him on a tiger hunt in the basement; is that correct—let him kill the tiger?'

"'To empower him.'"

"Some psychology," Lynne mumbled and started reading where I left off.

"Charlie said, 'You encouraged the parents to act out metaphorically that they were helping the child kill Brother Keith; is that correct?'

"'I'm sorry, it was a lion. To kill the lion that represented him. . . . It has been my experience in therapy that it does empower the child. . . . It's a way of them expressing their anger.'"

"Keith, Shirley Williams was therapist for four of the seven boys. Did she record or video any sessions?"

"No, and if you remember right, Charlie asked her about her skimpy notes in the preliminary hearing. 'I'm sure it's here someplace. Ah, here it is,' she said. 'I [wrote] the essence of the conversation.'

"Charlie then reminded her, 'You indicated on direct examination that as a therapist you do ask leading questions and don't see any part of your job as an investigator or attempting to get evidence for the police; is that correct?'

"'That's correct,' she agreed, '. . . My job is to work with the children therapeutically.'"

"I remember that now," Lynne said, "She almost looked panicky when Charlie handed her the exhibit which she identified as her initial intake report on which she had written her goals. I remember how exasperated she was when she identified the writing as her own and read, 'Continue gathering evidence for the police.'"

I looked at my wife and smiled. "Charlie led her on until she contradicted herself. That man is one smart lawyer."

Chapter 9

"Experts" on the Hot Seat

"Not once did Dr. Monteleone or Ms. LaRock tell the police that these findings could have 50 other causes."

We were well into the New Year, 1988, still transcribing the video interviews from Cardinal Glennon Hospital, hoping that a trial date would soon be set. It had now been almost 14 months since the police first knocked on my door. One day over lunch I explained to Andy, "The holdup on setting a trial date is in finding a judge to hear the case. They're all disqualifying themselves for one reason or another."

A crooked smile cracked Andy's face. "Smart judges don't want to risk their reputations."

"No, I'm sure they don't," I agreed. "But that's only part of my news."

"Keep talking, Little Preacher, I'm all ears."

"I just dropped some transcripts by the law office this morning. Bill Seibel presented me with an interesting question. Mr. Zimmerman from the prosecutor's office called them and wanted to know if I'd be willing to take an Alford plea on two counts before Judge Dugan."

"Alford plea, eh? Sounds like the prosecution's having a hard time making a case. So what's the bargain?"

"They'd ask for probation and have me go around and make talks about the evils of child molestation. The problem is, taking the plea will never clear my name. They have assumed I'm guilty and they're offering me a way to bail out; it's that or prove I'm innocent."

"Sound's like a back door exit for someone facing more charges than they're able to defend themselves against."

"It is. Bill explained that about 95 percent of all cases are settled on a plea bargaining basis to avoid the risk and expense of a trial when the amount of evidence makes the risk of conviction high and defense costly. Seibel thinks Mr. Zimmerman's probably looking for a way out of court that his boss, Mr. Hannah and I both might accept."

"So what are you going to do?" Andy asked, squinting at me through his cigarette smoke.

"I'm not going to roll over and play dead. I'm going to court."

"Fine," Andy said, "I'll be there, and if they do ship you off to the state pen in Jeff City, I'll visit you every weekend. I'll even keep you supplied in cigarettes for trading and give you a blow dryer to keep your hair straight."

"Yeah, right, just what I need." We both laughed.

"Have you talked with Charlie today?" Lynne asked her usual question when I came home one day. She was sitting on the floor transcribing a video.

"Charlie told me Bill Hannah's requesting a special prosecutor."

"Can he do that?"

"Sure, just like he requested a grand jury and didn't get it. One judge said his request was groundless. Also, Charlie says in Missouri it has to be an unusual case to merit a special prosecutor."

"Doesn't Hannah know that?"

"Maybe. One thing's sure. 'Grand jury' and 'special prosecutor' tagged to my name maintains negative press."

"I guess we're getting used to that." Lynne stood and stretched. "I've started transcribing the video of Tish LaRock's therapy sessions at Cardinal Glennon Hospital. Both she and Dr. Monteleone teach in training sessions for mandated reporters in the state." The phone rang and Lynne went to answer it. "It's for you, Keith, Laura Rogers."

"I thought you'd like to hear what Dr. Monteleone had to say at the Missouri Child Abuse and Neglect Conference."

"Sure, if it's interesting."

"I'll quote some of what Dr. Monteleone said as he was showing slides from other cases."

"'We used to think these injuries [from sexual abuse] were forever. We realize now that many of them go away. . . . A child with a gross tear—two weeks later [it is] gone. . . . This child is healed or you switched children on us. . . .'"[13]

"Since when does scar tissue heal, or is Monteleone claiming miraculous healing?" Charlie commented when I told him later. "What's more interesting, though is that Tish

LaRock testified in a deposition that she's aware of two cases where a mixup may have occurred at Cardinal Glennon Hospital.

"I've deposed three of the boys today," he said. "Remember the stick Mrs. Gaylord claimed you jabbed in Tim's rectum? When I questioned Tim today he said the stick was three feet long. It didn't hurt very much so he didn't cry, and there wasn't any blood.

"Alex said the pins you stuck in his legs were pretend. In fact, most of what the boys said today contradicted with previous statements. Things the boys claimed before that happened outside, now they're saying happened inside. They're changing their stories. They're now claiming things you haven't even been charged with."

As the weeks passed one of our greatest concerns, however, involved the admissibility of "hearsay evidence." Charlie and I discussed the issue many times. There was no way we could prove the parents were repeating verbatim what their children said to them.

Charlie explained, "The Missouri Supreme Court has ruled hearsay evidence admissible in cases like yours and we are beating a dead horse to try and keep it out. But we'll keep trying anyway."

Lynne had two outlets for her stress: One, her nursing made her actively focus on others and provided her with interested and caring friends. Her other was dance. She put on a Strauss tape, turned the volume high and did ballet exercises. Since losing my golfing partner, Ben Dole, I had hardly taken any time off, except for an occasional lunch with Andy or a fellow pastor. When home, both Lynne and I continued to spend most of our spare minutes in front of our TV transcribing videos and studying transcripts.

We now knew the strength of the prosecutor's case rested on the testimony of two people locally regarded as experts in sexual child abuse cases. These were Tish LaRock and Dr. James Monteleone.

In both her deposition and at the preliminary hearing, Tish LaRock mentioned her schooling, her work to help start the Sexual Abuse Management team at Cardinal Glennon Hospital in 1979, her sex abuse training from psychologists and social workers, independent reading, and practical experience. Ms. LaRock could mention no names of the professionals she'd trained under and cited only one publication by name which she had studied. However, she claimed to have interviewed "approximately 4,500 children."

"Is schooling and experience enough to qualify someone as an expert?" Lynne asked one day.

"I'm afraid some people think so, but Charlie gave me a quote he picked up from somewhere having to do with experts that I think is excellent. I shared it with Lynne.

"'Experience . . . is not enough to move from conjecture to science. . . . Controlled testing of ideas through research is necessary to be sure that one's experience is not filled with incorrect notions that go unrecognized . . . Thousands of women underwent radical mastectomy, . . . only subsequent research demonstrated that a simple mastectomy saves as many lives.'[14]

"So a person can practice chop sticks an hour a day," I observed, "but if they practice wrong, they will play it perfectly wrong."

I began reading Charlie's questioning of Tish LaRock to Lynne from the deposition transcript.

"'What is the procedure in the proper technique that you use and that you [use in] training other nurses in interviewing young children?'

"'. . . Not to lead the children to say something that is not true.' To the same question during the trial she clarified '. . . . Not suggesting an answer to them or asking them leading questions. . . . The child needs to be put at ease, [in] talking. . . . Ask them about different body parts, . . . use an anatomically correct doll and assess their knowledge, . . . their concept of privacy of genital parts and see if they know anything about sexual abuse or . . . prevention skills.'

"'Once you make your findings, Ms. LaRock, you don't make any sort of medical or psychological conclusions, do you?'

"'Well, we are placed in a position where we have to make some assessment whether we think the child has been abused, . . . We usually make that as a team.'"

Lynne arched her eyebrows. "Still the head of the department is ultimately accountable."

"Yes, and Monteleone's supposed to be head of the SAM unit, but each one should be held accountable. Instead they are all immune," I replied and started thumbing through a copy of his deposition.

"Listen to this, Lynne. Charlie said, 'I'd like to go on record for the jury to know that Dr. Monteleone is refusing to provide any authoritative sources to back up his statements, and he's refusing to provide [reports from Dr.] Woodling, who he claims is an authoritative source; he's refusing, and he's specifically stating he does not even know what his textbooks are when he teaches a class.'"

I read the part where Charlie Bridges questioned Monteloeine about the funneling condition he claimed to have found in the anus of one of the boys.

"'How mnay boys have you observed funneling in?' Charlie asked.

"'I didn't keep track. We're trying to accumulate that data now, but I have no knowledge of it offhand.'

"'And who is trying to accumulate that data?'

"'We are. We're trying to computerize it and do some computerized studies so we can get those figures when we want them.'

"'At what stage is that computerization at?'

"'Stage zero. We got the computer.'"

"Monteleone sounded as if documentation couldn't be done without a computer," Lynne commented. I resumed reading Charlie's interrogation of the doctor.

"'So you don't know of any group that is currently preparing standards as to properly diagnosing sexual abuse in children?'

"'Not offhand.'

"'Do you have any procedure manual at the SAM clinic for the unit?'

"'No, . . . it's taught by word of mouth.'"

"As accurate as gossip, I'm sure," Lynne interrupted. I kept on reading the responses of Dr. Monteleone to Charlie's questioning.

"'Of the children you saw in 1986, how many did you put in your report [that] were not sexually abused?'

"'We never say not sexually abused. We never use that term. We say SAM evaluation.'"

Lynne turned to me in disgust. "Keith, that says nothing. It's like a patient asking what their CAT scan shows and the doctor answers 'CAT Scan.'"

"I know," I shrugged and turned back to the transcript and the demonstration of Charlie's ability to paint the prosecution's expert into a corner.

"'So you never put in a report that a child was not sexually abused?'

"'You can never say they've not been sexually abused; never. . . . The system decides that; we don't. . . . Often, we were having trouble in the courtroom [getting convictions because] we found nothing physically wrong; we were told to do that so we could remind them that even though there is no physical finding that the child is abused.'

"'Who told you to do that?'

"'The legal system.'

"'The prosecuting attorneys told you to do that, didn't they?'

"'Yes.'"

"You know, Keith," Lynne almost shouted, "the kids, the parents, and you, you're all victims of a bureaucratic monster. I wonder how many people get caught in the same trap each year? I think I came across some figures in the depositions."

Lynne reached for the transcript of Charlie's deposition of Dr. Monteleone and I picked up Ms. LaRock's. Lynne started reading first.

"'Has the number of children seen by the SAM clinic increased every year since you've been the director?'

"'Yes, it has, . . .like 200 . . . and now it's about 1,200. That parallels all national figures, Missouri, and everywhere.'

"'Are there any hospitals in St. Louis other than Cardinal Glennon, that see as many as 1,200 children in a year for sexual abuse?'

"'No.'"

"I see here, Lynne, that Tish LaRock's deposition compliments Monteleone's. In 1987 she estimated that between a thousand and a thousand and fifty sexually abused children were brought to the SAM unit at Cardinal Glennon. She saw approximately half of those. A good number of those cases, she said, were referred by Social Services to help in their evaluation.'

"Look, Lynne, Charlie next asked Ms. LaRock about one of the therapists." I started reading.

"'Did you refer [the children involved] to Shirley Williams? . . . And you were aware that she was not a psychologist or a psychiatrist?'

"'Yes.'

"'Were you aware at the time that she is not a licensed therapist?'

"'No.'

"'Do you have any knowledge of the type of therapy that she employs with young children?'

"'Specifically I would say no. . . .'"

"What does Charlie have to say about all this, Keith?" Lynne asked.

I read to Lynne some notes from a conversation I'd had with Charlie. "'I've never seen the Division of Family Service's workers in St. Charles County have the child examined by anyone other than Cardinal Glennon. Most of the false allegations I see come up in kids interviewed a lot where kids say it didn't happen and the interviewer makes up their mind it did. I see a lot of it coming from the same doctor and therapists. It's a system where the police and the DFS have learned which hospital will more likely support allegations of abuse.'"

By comparing the testimonies of Dr. Monteleone and Tish LaRock we got a picture of how the system worked. Both professionals said that a team of three, the nurse, social worker, and doctor, determined if abuse occurred. In the preliminary hearing Dr.Monteleone explained further, "There are three aspects of the whole system . . .And all three of them play a very essential role. Most important is what the child says. . . . The history, a good detailed history by the child saying what happened. Secondly, does the child have any behavioral indicators? Then, three, you see the physical findings."

Lynne read from Dr. Monteleone's deposition, "'As a rule, . . . no real typical medical history is done.'

"That's an understatement," my nurse wife commented. "A detailed medical history is mandatory to rule out any other medical possibility." Lynne picked up on Charlie's questioning of Dr. Monteleone in the preliminary hearing.

"'Dr. Monteleone, you realize that many of these kids were being treated by pediatricians prior to coming to see you, don't you?'

"'Yes, sir.'

"'Did you obtain those medical reports from their pediatricians prior to them coming to see you?'

"'No, I didn't.'"

As Lynne and I transcribed the hospital videos, we realized Ms. LaRock's interviews of the children were a softened version of the police interviews. She never scolded or threatened the children for lying, she simply refused to let the children go until she had the information she wanted. One child continually rubbed his eyes, complaining about being tired and wanting to go home. Todd was hungry and wanted to eat, "Now can I have something to eat?" he kept asking. LaRock kept promising, "after a few more" questions. She interviewed Todd three times in one day.

In her interviews, Ms. LaRock often ignored answers by a child and constantly repeated questions until she got a statement supporting abuse. Praise like, "Very good," and "You know all the answers, don't you," throughout the interviews, clued the children to provide acceptable answers. She justified herself in the preliminary hearing by saying, "I think sometime if a child—if I need to understand and make sure the child understands my question, I'll repeat it in a different way."

"She's contradicted herself," Lynne pointed out when I read Ms. LaRock's statement. "She testified in her deposition that she instructed other nurses to 'just accept what the child is able to say.'"

It seemed apparent to us that Ms. LaRock listened to the parents' suspicions, interviewed the children, and then wrote up her interpretation of what she recalled. Not once in her written reports did she mention their constant denials.

"Yes," Lynne added, "and those comments became the child's 'history' of abuse. So Dr. Monteleone and LaRock could refer to the children having a 'history' of child abuse and most everyone would assume they were referring to the usual 'medical history' a doctor accumulates when he treats a patient for illness or disease."

We noticed that in videos of the first interviews, all the children denied that anything had happened to them, but Dr. Monteleone, we found, had an answer for that too. Lynne pointed out, "Keith, look how he explained the common opinion about denials," and she read Dr. Montelone's answer to Charlie from the court record.

"'. . . So, it's not unusual for children who have been sexually abused . . . to deny it happened.'

"'Is it unusual for children who have not been sexually abused to deny that it's happened?'

"'Yeah. That's true too.'"

I studied through more materials late in the evenings when the children were in bed and Lynne was working. I discovered that both LaRock and the doctor talked a lot about the children's fears. In discussing Tim Raymond, Dr. Monteleone testified in deposition, "He was very distraught, and very upset."

"So when you were, what, touching him or doing the physical exam, he was very distraught?" Charlie asked.

"He was resistant and very upset."

"When your medical record said that he was very cooperative and alert?"

"Maybe the term resistant is—apprehensive might be the better answer for that. These children were all apprehensive and very frightened children, but they cooperated."

"... You're telling us one thing, and opposite things in your report; isn't that correct?"

"There isn't anything in what I said," Monteleone replied.

"Assume, [Dr. Monteleone] that the police interview of this child was consistent denials, that the Cardinal Glennon [Hospital] interview of this child was consistent denials, that your physical exam of this child was, I think you [called it] 'not remarkable,' but you still conclude that the child has been sexually abused, based upon the behavior indicators. . . . Let me ask you about these behavioral indicators. Is it unusual for a child to have night terrors, sleep disorders, fears of falling asleep?"

"Not at all."

Charlie read a statement from Dr. Anthony Rostain. "'Sleep disorders are common during childhood and vary according to the age of the child, . . . preschoolers have difficulties falling and staying asleep, night terrors, nightmares, and enuresis. . . .

"I'm asking you, [Dr. Monteleone] to explain if you went through the normal medical diagnosis in this case, to rule out various things such as bedtime routine, family stresses, or history of sleep disorders, did you do any of those things in diagnosing this sleep disorder as being connected with sexual abuse?"

"No. I felt it was strongly due to sexual abuse."

"And is it common for you, Doctor, not to, or is it common for you to make a diagnosis without ruling out other causes for that diagnosis?"

"... Everyone knows in a situation in medicine you can list 50 things that causes just about anything."

"... A good physician doesn't even question the family

about medical history of other problems?"

"Not when he has—if it walks like a duck and quacks like a duck, it's a duck."

Charlie further asked Monteleone in the preliminary hearing, "And who is better qualified in your opinion to identify behavioral indicators that are caused by sexual abuse, a pediatrician, or a psychiatrist, or psychologist?"

"A pediatrician who deals with the problem extensively."

"Such as yourself?"

"Yes."

When Lynne came home that evening she was particularly curious to see what Dr. Monteleone and Ms. LaRock had to say about physical findings. In Charlie's deposition of Ms. LaRock, she stated that she thought it would be harmful to a sexually abused child for a doctor to test the laxity of the sphincter muscles by inserting a finger into the rectum. She described SAM's method. Lynne read LaRock's testimony to me.

"'Well, some of the children—when we examine them just visually, looking at the anal opening, you can determine if there is a laxity or not. Some of the children that have been abused over a period of time really have a relaxed response to someone looking in that area and you can see a dilation of that opening that you just don't see normally in a regular physical examination or in the children that haven't been anally abused. You can see a dilation and a relaxed state that really normally isn't there.'"

Not once did Dr. Monteleone or Ms. LaRock tell the police or the parents that these findings could have 50 other causes. Instead they used the terms "consistent with" and people not familiar with the term thought it meant the same as a definite diagnosis.

"I've been trying to remember all evening," Lynne said one night when she came home from work, "what Dr. Monteleone said about his method of documentation."

"I highlighted it, Lynne. I'll find it and read it to you." After she'd changed her clothes she sat beside me and I started reading more examination of Dr. Monteleone by Charlie during the preliminary hearing.

"'How did you document the funneling? Do you have any methods of—?'

"'No. It's an eyeball thing.'

"'Dilation is alone sufficient for you to conclude positively that a child had been anally penetrated?'

"'Yes, . . . if the dilation is sufficient.'

"'What is sufficient enough?'

"'The figure they give is greater than 1.5 milligrams.'*

"'And did you put any measurements down in your report as far as dilation—?'

"' . . . Usually I will put down, 'is greater than.' You put a number down and numbers mean nothing to people.'

"'They mean things to doctors, don't they?'

"'Not necessarily.'"

Lynne's medical training came bursting out in a rush of anger and shock. "Keith, in medicine, something hasn't happened unless it's seen, measured, described, or illustrated. If it's not documented, it didn't happen."

Lynne sat silent and rigid while I kept reading Charlie's grilling of Dr. Monteleone on other physical findings. Then he shifted his questions slightly. "Is it medically possible to place green beans and corn in a child's penis?'

"'Yes, I think it would be.'

"'You think it would be? Could you explain that to us, how you would place green beans and corn inside a four-year-old child's penis?'

"Lynne, this is where Zimmerman objected." I read his objection to her.

"'Your Honor, I don't think this witness is qualified—well, I'll withdraw it.'

"And Charlie said, 'If he wants to say he is not qualified, we can strike his entire testimony.'"

Early in July Charlie called with important news. "The State Supreme Court," he said, "has appointed Frank Conley, a circuit court judge from Columbia to be your trial judge. He has a reputation for giving stiff sentences. And they say he hates child abusers."

I gulped when I heard that.

"He's also known for his fairness."

"He'll be here on the 29th and 30th to hear more pretrial motion testimony," Charlie continued. "I'm going to present

---

*   The transcript says "milligrams." However the
       doctor might have meant "millimeters."

a motion to deny the admissability of hearsay evidence. Primarily, Zimmerman will have to prove the reliability of the hearsay testimony."

At 8:25 a.m. on the day appointed, Judge Conley walked into the courtroom, his demeanor demanding respect like James Stewart or Gregory Peck. He flashed a warm smile and surprised me when he extended his hand. "I'm Frank Conley," he said. I liked him. After the hearing, the judge called the defense and prosecuting attorneys into his chambers.

Later Charlie informed me, "Judge Conley told John Zimmerman he had a Mickey Mouse law suit here and Zimmerman had a lot of problems with the case. Conley also told Zimmerman he needed to decide if he really wanted to proceed with all the charges or if he wanted to drop most of the charges and go with his best ones. Then he looked at both of us and said, 'This trial will not drag on longer than a week.'

"Conley will review the entire case, videos, investigation reports, everything. Then he'll rule on the admissability of hearing evidence and set a trial date. It won't be long now until we go to court for the big one. I only hope he gives us enough time to present an adequate defense."

Early in August I took a check from my legal defense fund to Charlie's office and found him in his law library. He was busy putting together materials in my case to send to Judge Conley.

"Charlie, I just talked to Carol Marks, the counselor from California—remember, she was the lady who called me some time ago and sent us so much helpful information. She's been following closely the McMartin Pre-school case in L.A."

"Yes, I've been keeping up with that case myself in the newspapers. There appears to be a lot of similarity there with yours. Two of the prosecutors out there have resigned and a third one was fired after he said he didn't believe the state had a real case. What did Ms. Marks say?"

"She said that hearsay testimony is not allowed in California."

"Well, Reverend, every state is different. I'll still do everything I can to get the judge here to disallow hearsay."

I left Charlie's office thankful for his tenacity.

About a month later, Charlie let me know that Zimmerman had filed amended information on charges against me. "He now has 19 counts," Charlie said. "We've got to have the best defense possible. I've decided to fly to California to consult with Dr. Coleman."

Charlie saw the doctor on September 12. I went over to his office shortly after he got back.

"Ordinarily my concern as a defense attorney is to keep harmful information out of court," Charlie explained. "However, after talking with Dr. Coleman, it appears our best defense is to allow everything, including the hearsay testimonies, into the trial. We want the jury to hear what the children, parents, and therapists are claiming." Charlie leaned back in his chair and smiled confidently. "By comparing the dates of the various interviews and therapy sessions, we can show that the kids didn't make accusations until after they were asked leading questions. We can show how the children were led into making these false allegations.

About a week later Charlie called to give me the trial date, October 24, 1988.

Chapter Ten

My Trial Begins

"All anybody ever hears is that children don't lie about these things."

Late one night the answering machine clicked on. An accented male voice spoke slowly, as if he were reading a script. "Mr. Barnhart, I know you're home, and I've been though your house already. I know where your kids live at, sleep at, and you and your wife sleep at. I'm gonna kill ya before y'er trial comes up and all the people in the congregation's gonna die 'cause I'm gonna blow 'em all off the face of the earth."

I turned on the bedside lamp and watched the color drain from Lynne's face. "These people are desperate, Keith."

"I know, and desperate people don't do rational things."

"You're right," Lynne agreed, "and for the first time in my life I'm learning to trust—hourly. My relationship with God is the only thing keeping me sane."

I called Charlie the next morning and he advised I report the threat to the sheriff's department. They suggested a telephone tap. Tensions kept mounting as the trial date loomed near. I was in my office when Lynne phoned. Her voice was edged with anxiety. "I've been trying to reach you, Keith. Mother called. You know how much trouble she's been having with Dad and his awful Alzheimer's Disease. Mother says he's been a lot worse. Lately, she's been up day and night with him. I feel awful leaving you and the children right now, but Mother needs help until she can find a nursing home for him. What should I do?"

"We'll manage. Go be with your family." Lynne prepared immediately to fly to New Orleans.

I opened my Bible to Isaiah, chapter 26 and read, "The steadfast in mind, I will keep in perfect peace, because he trusts in thee. Trust in the Lord forever, for in God the Lord, we have an everlasting rock." Fortunately, they were able to place Lynne's father in a suitable nursing home almost immediately and Lynne returned home in four days.

One month before the trial Charlie called. "I've got news. The State's going to dismiss 17 of the 19 counts against you." I was speechless.

After a brief pause Charlie explained, "John Zimmerman sent three copies of all the reports off for other opinions. He sent one to the FBI and the other two copies to two nationally recognized psychologists, Nancy Aldrich in Georgia and Eileen Tracy in New York. These two experts and the FBI all told him there's no case. In my opinion, Zimmerman wants to dismiss all counts but Bill Hannah won't let him."

"Why not?" I found my voice.

"Probably because Hannah's publicly stated there was enough evidence to prosecute," Charlie replied.

I found it hard to concentrate on work the rest of the day.

Harold Hendrick and other pastor friends organized a prayer rally at my church for October 14, ten days before my trial was scheduled to start. Lynne and I lost count of the number of people who came and hugged us and said, "We love you and we're standing with you." It was especially gratifying for me to see longstanding friends from DeSoto in the congregation. Some of them had known me since I was a child in Sunday School at my home church.

To date over $50,000 had been received toward my legal expenses, much of it tucked into letters of encouragement. One particularly touching note came from a third grade girl who wrote, "I know you didn't do it. I'm very sorry. I would walk across hot coals for you. I can't wait till this is over. Love, Shannon."

The dropping of most of the counts and the support of so many dear people helped ease our fears. Still, we knew that despite my innocence I could be sent to prison for a long term.

It was now only days before the trial. As I had so many times during the past 21 months, I stopped again at Charlie and Bill's law office. I had an important decision to make.

"Before we get down to the business at hand," Charlie said, "I want to tell you that Dr. Coleman and Dr. ten Bensel have reviewed your case and are ready to speak in your defense. They'll be here on the trial date. Dr. Coleman will testify to the psychological leading of the children and Dr. ten Bensel will be our medical expert.

"Now, Reverend, you've got to decide between a judge and a jury. The law provides the right to a trial by jury. However, the defendant may choose to have only a judge." We discussed my options for a few minutes, then Charlie said, "I was impressed with Judge Conley's no-nonsense approach, having met him at a hearing, but I'm worried about his reported strong feelings toward child abusers. Well, the decision is yours."

I took off my glasses and rubbed my eyes. I thought for a minute and said, "Charlie, I think I'd feel better placing my future in the hands of 12 people rather than just one."

Charlie leaned back in his black leather chair and managed a tight smile. "That's probably the best way to go."

Lynne's sister, Leanna arrived Sunday evening, October 23. All we could talk about was the trial starting the next morning. For over 21 months I had declared my innocence and tomorrow I was finally going to court.

"How does it look for you, Keith," Leanna asked after Matthew and Emily were settled in bed. Leanna was familiar with the issues because we had sent her copies of some of the videos and transcripts.

"One of the biggest advantages I have is the total unity of the Child Care workers. Their stories are consistent and their reputations can't be questioned. With the variations in all their work schedules, as well as the open door policy of the Child Care, they know there's no way I could have done what I'm charged for. If the jury will hear the evidence—" I paused a moment and shook my head. "Leanna, we can't be certain. At least two of the little boys are going to take the stand. There's no way to predict the verdict. All anybody ever hears is that children don't lie about these things."

"Yeah," Leanna said, "but any parent knows that children like to give you the answers you want to hear. I know that mine will."

"That's the dogma," I sighed. "And that's probably our biggest problem. Besides everybody's heart goes out to the seven little boys whose stories are said to be supported by quote 'medical experts.'"

Lynne joined the conversation. "Not only that, since 17 charges involving the other five boys have been dropped, a major part of our evidence may not be admitted."

Leanna summed it up for both of us: "So the outcome of the trial isn't really certain."

"That's about it," I answered wearily. "Only God is." The three of us prayed together and went to bed.

Monday morning set our routine for the week. We took Emily and Matthew to school a little earlier than usual, then stopped by Hardee's for coffee to go. We drove to the now familiar domed St. Charles County Courthouse. We hoped to be early enough to get a parking place in the mini-lot which crowns the ridge overlooking historic Main Street where the first capital building of Missouri still stands. We had only a few minutes to sip our coffee before the trial began at 8:30.

Charlie, Bill Seibel, and I walked into the courtroom first, entering through large glass-paneled doors on the left and taking seats at the table where the defendant and his attorneys always sat. Lynne and Leanna; a crowd of our friends; the prosecuting parents, their sons, and supporters; a few morbid sensation seekers; and the day's anticipated witnesses had to wait in the lobby until after the jury selection was completed. Most of the media had not arrived yet.

This was the first time I had been in this main courtroom. Four tall, wood-framed, weighted windows stretched toward the high ceiling with narrow faded rose drapes drooping along each side. I felt as if I had walked onto a Perry Mason TV set.

While we waited for the selection of jurors to begin Charlie shared some facts that weren't very comforting. "Jury selection is one of the hardest parts in a trial like yours. You try to see if there is anyone who has a definite bias. It's hard for some people to admit they are biased because they don't want to be knocked off the jury. It ends up being a lot of guess work."

Ordinarily, 50 jury candidates would have been in the pool, Charlie said. This was no ordinary trial, 125 had been called up. The winnowing process took the entire morning. Judge Conley, Prosecuting Attorney Zimmerman, and finally my chief attorney, Charlie Bridges, asked questions of the candidates to weed out "biased" jurists. By the middle of the afternoon fresh air was blowing through the opened windows relieving the warm stuffiness. Only twelve acceptable jurists, plus two alternates now remained. As I scanned their unfamiliar faces, I felt a chill of cold reality creep through me. These twelve strangers would decide my future.

When we were dismissed for a half hour break, I joined Lynne, Leanna, and our friends who were still waiting in the lobby. The two little boys who had been brought to testify against me saw me clearly and showed no fear or apprehension. At one time Tim Raymond was less than five feet from me. Lynne and I tried to ignore the boys and their parents as we sipped hot chocolate from a machine and made small talk with friends. The half hour passed quickly and it was time for the proceedings to begin.

Lynne and Leanna entered with me and took a seat in an oak pew directly behind the oak rail that ran across the whole courtroom to the jury box on the opposite side, just to the right of where the prosecution sat. The rail separated the spectator section from the trial principals. Lynne couldn't quite touch me, but I knew she was there.

At 3:25 p.m. the deputy clerk swore in the jurists and Judge Conley asked for the State's opening statement. John Zimmerman, slender and slightly taller than me, had only to stand and turn to his right to face the jury close-up. He stood at ease and began as if he were the announcer in a boxing ring.

"We have a fascinating case for you, Ladies and Gentlemen, we really do. In one corner we have little boys. . . ." He introduced to the jury Todd Brady, now six years old. "He'll testify that Brother Keith took him upstairs from the Day Care Center, . . . pulled his pants down, [and] touched his penis.

"Now Ladies and Gentlemen, words like that are going to be used in this trial. . . . That's what this case is all about." I carefully studied the jurors' faces. They were bland and frozen, less revealing than wax models in Madam Toussant's museums.

"The second child, [Tim Raymond], a little blond-headed boy, is going to testify that Brother Keith took him out of the . . . Day Care Center, brought him upstairs and outside, took him on a walk, [and] that he had another little friend with him." Zimmerman drew a deep breath and paused, dramatically lowering his voice, then continued. . . . "During that walk Brother Keith pulled his [Tim's] pants down, took a branch and put that branch in Tim's rectal area, in his anus.

"It's not going to be very pretty testimony, Ladies and Gentlemen, but it will be coming from the mouths of five- and six-year-old children." Mr. Zimmerman then promised that their parents would testify along with Detective Pope, and the nurse and the doctor from Cardinal Glennon Hospital.

"Now, Ladies and Gentlemen, the State needs to prove [the defendant's guilt] to you beyond a reasonable doubt. It's our burden of proof [that] the defendant is guilty of sexual abuse in the first degree on Todd Brady, that he subjected Todd Brady, a person less than 12 years old, to sexual contact by touching the victim's penis with his hand.

"In Count Two, the State must prove to you the defendant is guilty of abuse of a child with regard to Tim Raymond, that the defendant knowingly inflicted cruel and inhuman punishment on Tim Raymond, a child less than 17 years old, by placing a foreign object in his rectum and in the course there of the defendant caused serious emotional injury to Tim Raymond. . . . I think when you look at this evidence you will return no other verdict than guilty. Thank you."

A slight stirring rustled through the courtroom as the prosecutor took his seat. Judge Conley looked toward Charlie, seated at my table on the left. Our table was directly in front of the courtroom doors, and to the judge's right.

Charlie stepped over toward the jury. Without a touch of drama in either voice or actions he methodically began the preview of my case. "One of our first witnesses that we're going to call is going to be Dr. Lee Coleman. He's a child psychologist from Berkeley, California." Charlie expounded on Dr. Coleman's impressive credentials and experience. "He's published approximately forty articles [in] books . . . and common magazines that you all are aware of, Psychology Today, U.S. News and World Report—to very specific psychiatric magazines.

"[Dr. Coleman] will bring up that children between the ages of three and six are very susceptible to being suggested to, . . . there's not any studies that dispute this." Charlie spent more time introducing the topics Dr. Coleman would address. He promised video tapes of Ms. Tish LaRock which showed her ignoring the denials of children. "It's nowhere in her reports, but it's all over the videotapes," Charlie said.

"The first witness we are going to call to show you how the case developed and how these principles go into effect. . . . How these parents first came to believe their child was sexually abused. . . . Mrs. Walker [one of the parents] will tell you that she started calling other families, other parents saying, 'I think my son has been abused at school, maybe you better talk to your children and see if they've been abused.' For example, she will tell them that 'if your son has bad dreams, . . . starts talking baby talk, that's proof your child has been abused.'"

It soon became evident that Charlie's strategy was to present in his opening statement pertinent information that would not be admitted as evidence, since 17 of the 19 counts had been dropped.

Zimmerman apparently recognized what was happening and kept making objections. Many were overruled. Charlie pressed on.

". . . I will introduce . . . a videotape statement of Chad Walker. He was the first one [the police] talked to. . . . I'll let you decide if any leading or suggestive questions were asked. . . . We will introduce the video tape of Curtis Farrow where the police asked him every leading suggestion you can think of. And he continually denies."

Charlie further promised a video of a group interview of four boys, even though Dr. Monteleone had claimed group interviews were never done at Cardinal Glennon Hospital. Charlie also said he would show evidence that it was Todd's parents and the professionals who suggested Brother Keith touched Todd's penis, and prove that for over three months Todd made more than fifteen denials and since his one accusation, had made denials again."

I looked at my watch. Charlie had been dodging Zimmerman's interruptions for over an hour, promising evidence that would prove how my case really hinged on the snowballing panic started by Keri Walker. A panic that gathered momentum through reports from therapists and police interviews, sensationalized by the media, particularly Channel Five of St. Louis.

It was two hours before Charlie completed his statement. After Judge Conley dismissed the jury at 5:45, Prosecutor Zimmerman unleashed his fury. He charged that Charlie's statement contained prejudicial information that tainted the jury. He moved that evidence pertaining to anything but the two charges being tried not be allowed in court. Although Judge Conley postponed a ruling, Zimmerman's motion made my spirits sag, but at least the jury knew we were not witholding any evidence. We had no reason to do so.

Andy Mueller sidled up to me as we left the courtroom. "I've never seen Mr. Bridges try a case before, but I'll tell you what, he can charm flies away from a spider, and he's not shifty. He's good." Andy had a way of encouraging me.

Lynne, Leanna, and I picked up Emily and Matthew from the friend's house where they had been staying. It had been a long day and we were thankful for the supper brought by a church family.

At 8:20 Tuesday morning the State called Tim Raymond for their first witness. The little towhead six year old almost skipped to the witness stand, while his mother, Mrs. Gaylord sat facing him from her seat close by the prosecution's table.

Zimmerman began. "Tim, I have to have you stand up and raise your right hand. Will you do that, please?"

"I don't know it," Tim innocently exclaimed, trying to decide which hand to raise. After a little assistance from the prosecutor Tim was sworn in. He looked so small as he scrunched into the big green witness chair, his tiny legs dangling over the edge. He could remember neither his last name nor the name of the school he attended nearly two years before where the alleged abuse was supposed to have taken place.

"Do you remember a guy named Brother Keith at the school?"

"Un-huh."

"O.K. Do you see him here today? Is he around here somewhere? Look around to everybody. . . . Is he here . . . ? Why don't you point to him for me." Little Tim's dangling legs came to a standstill as he stretched tall in his chair and pointed a finger at me. His face glowed with satisfaction, not fear.

Charlie took over for the cross-examination. His demeanor was unthreatening as he gently proceeded to question Tim.

"Did they tell you that you should say that God helps you remember?"

Tim nodded his head.

"Who told you to say God helps you remember. . . ?

"Mom and Dad."

"And do you sometimes have trouble remembering what Brother Keith did to you?"

"Yeah."

"Who helps you remember?"

"Mommy and Mr. Zimmerman."

"Did they help you remember that when Brother Keith put a stick in your bottom that it hurt?"

"Yeah." Mrs. Gaylord's quiet sobbing was becoming more distracting with each answer Tim gave. Charlie had been trying to prove to the jury that the boy could be easily led into a number of contradictions. I wondered if the jury heard the discrepancies or if they only felt sympathy for Tim's mother.

Todd Brady approached the stand slightly less confident, although his father accompanied him. He testified much like Zimmerman said he would, but when Charlie cross-examined him, his dad acted nervous.

"Do you remember . . . . when you and your Daddy played a game and he pretended that he was Brother Keith. . .?"

"Yeah."

"O.K. Who pulled your pants down when you went into the room that time?"

"Dad."

". . . And why did he pull your pants down?"

"Because we were practicing. . . ."

Charlie then asked questions about Todd's visits with therapist Shirley Williams. "Did she let you play with those dolls?"

"Yes."

"What was the big man doll's name?"

"Brother Keith."

"And what was the little boy doll's name?"

"Todd."

"Todd, did Brother Keith ever stick any pins or needles in your legs?"

"No."

"He didn't really put pins in your legs, did he?"

"No."

Charles Gaylord, Tim's stepfather was the first parent to testify. He briskly stepped to the stand and casually draped his left arm over the railing. Ignoring the attorneys, he addressed all his answers to the judge and jury. The main thrust of his testimony centered around the stick incident which he went to the school to investigate. However, he admitted neither talking with the other boys nor the teacher whom Tim said were present at the time when the incident was supposed to have happened.

Lynne could hardly listen to him and later explained, "The only thing I could think of was the line in 'My Fair Lady' where Henry Higgins described a former student, 'Oozing charm from every pore, he oiled his way across the floor.'"

Zimmerman called Mrs. Gaylord. She walked to the stand fully composed, a contrast to her tearfulness during Tim's testimony. At the prosecutor's request, she described Channel Five's news feature in mid-December, 1986.

"... They had showed a picture of the Cave Springs Baptist Church and School. And they had said that if any parents had noticed any behavioral changes in their children and they attended that school to notify the police department as soon as possible. ... I was very upset."

She talked about coming to see me. "The muscles in [Brother Keith's] face ... quivered like they were about to pop out. ... I've never seen a human being that scared."

I leaned across the table to Charlie and whispered, "You would be too, if she threatened your life."

Mrs. Brady testified for Zimmerman that Todd had regularly wet his bed, since before attending the Child Care. Then during Charlie's cross-exam, she stated that Todd's accusations against me came after an interview session of leading questions. Mrs. Brady surprised me by her composure because she had appeared belligerent during the preliminary hearing.

It was late afternoon by the time Prosecutor Zimmerman put his expert witness, Dr. Monteleone on the stand. I was surprised, as at the preliminary hearing, that the doctor consulted no notes.

After reviewing Dr. Monteleone's training, Zimmerman asked his present status. "I'm on faculty at St. Louis University, stationed at Cardinal Glennon [Hospital]."

"And what exactly do you teach?"

"Pediatrics, endocrinology, and child abuse. ... In 1980 I took over the [SAM] team as chairman, ...my first exposure to sex abuse [was] probably [in the] early '80's." After the doctor estimated seeing over 2,000 sex abuse cases, Zimmerman asked him about his medical findings on each of the boys that had made allegations.

It was 6:20 in the evening before the direct examination was complete and Charlie moved to wait for the cross-exam until morning. I felt panic,—the jury would have the whole night to ponder only Monteleone's unrefuted testimony!

Wednesday morning we entered the court room feeling anxious. The jurists looked stoically past me, while some of my accusers glared with what appeared to be contempt and even hate. I was thankful for the warm smiles of devoted friends.

Dr. Monteleone again came to the stand without any obvious medical files or notes. Charlie began the cross-exam postponed from the night before. He first reviewed some of Dr. Monteleone's statements made during Zimmerman's direct exam the day before.

". . . Do you know of anyone who has seen more children than yourself in a clinical situation?" Charlie asked.

"No." Then he mentioned Astrid Heger in California as seeing about as many. In response to further questioning by Charlie, the doctor reiterated the usual procedures of the SAM unit and emphasized, "Usually our aim is to get a spontaneous declaration from the child without asking leading questions." I knew that none of the video taped interviews of the children backed this claim, but I feared that the jury would not be allowed to see them.

"We look at three things," Dr. Monteleone said, "what the child says; is it reasonable. . . ? [It] still comes down to do you believe the child. Second thing is, does the child have behavior indicators? . . . And then finally the physical findings." He talked more about terminology of child abuse accepted by the legal system and concluded, "At present, now, I decide if I feel a child has been sexually abused, I'll put down sexual abuse."

Dr. Monteleone testified to finding no remarkable physical findings on Todd, then described an anal scar he had found on Tim. "On Tim Raymond, . . . were you able to measure this scar?" Charlie asked.

"No. You don't measure. Impossible."

Because in previous testimony Monteleone claimed to have written and published articles, Charlie questioned him on these.

"I served you with a subpoena and asked you to bring every article, every paper you've ever written. Did you bring that with you today?"

"No, sir, I didn't." After repeated questioning and many side-stepping answers, Monteleone finally admitted that he had only published two papers, one in New Zealand and the other in Rio de Janeiro.

"Have [you ever published papers] in any authoritative [publication] such as in *Pediatrics* [or some other] authoritative textbook?"

"No, sir. . . ."

"Now, do you have in your report the size of the small scar that you saw on Tim's anus?"

"No, I do not, sir." When the doctor estimated the scar to be at least one centimeter long, Charlie pointed out that in his deposition he had testified that he did not know if the scar was less than a millimeter or greater than a millimeter. It had grown ten times between the testimonies.

"Is it consistent with reasonable medical procedure to not put in the size of the scar?"

"Sure," Monteleone answered with an air of confidence. Several minutes later he asked permission to draw the scar, which he did. He admitted the drawing was crude as he made a circle with a few vague scribbles around it.

"Let me ask you if this small scar can be caused by scratching?"

"It might be able to, yes, sir." After Charlie suggested other possible causes, Dr. Montelone said, "I think it's feasible to put a stick in the anus . . . and show no trauma whatsoever."

"Are you familiar with the A[merican] M[edical] A[ssociation] diagnostic and treatment guidelines. . . ?"

"Yes, I think I have seen that."

"There is a list of approximately 16 items, signs of sexual abuse, . . . difficulty in walking, sitting. . . . Did you have any history of that?"

"No, sir. Does it list also 'no findings?"

"No," Charlie answered.

"It doesn't list 'no findings,'" Dr. Monteleone explained, "because that's probably the greatest finding of all. No finding."

As soon as we had a break, I told Lynne, "Monteleone's logic reminds me of the flea principle: Pull two legs off a flea and tell it to jump, it jumps. Pull two more legs off and tell it to jump, it jumps. Pull the last two legs off and tell it to jump, and it sits there. Conclusion: if you pull all the legs off and tell it to jump, it goes deaf."

Ms. Tish LaRock was the State's next witness. Her shoulder length, straight, light brown hair blended with her colorless face and bland expression. With a controlled unemotional voice, she described her training and experience with the SAM unit and outlined the basic interview routine. She said she had completed a bachelor of science degree in nursing.

After she explained her method of questioning children suspected of having been abused, Zimmerman asked, "Do you view that particular technique as pressing the child to say something or manipulating and if not, why isn't that manipulating the child?"

"Well, I don't feel that it's manipulating the child because I'm not asking the question in a sense that we use that to make them change their story. Just to clarify. . . ."

". . . Do you believe that you manipulated Todd or Tim Raymond?"

"No, I don't."

As Charlie came to cross-examine Ms. LaRock, I wished that the jurists could only see her videos. Charlie was kind but unrelenting with her in cross-examination. "You testified at a preliminary hearing [in] September 1987. . . . 'I have . . . . a bachelor's degree in nursing,' didn't you?"

". . . I found out that there was a few more requirements . . . . before I could graduate."

"At a deposition you told me you had finished [your bachelor's degree] in May, 1988."

"That was my impression."

"And earlier in your testimony today you have said you completed your bachelor's degree but now you're telling us in fact . . . you haven't completed [it]?"

". . . There were some other things that I didn't know about. . . . They say I should graduate in May."

Charlie asked Ms. LaRock about Todd's behavior during her interview with him. "He seemed very [frigid]. Very frightened. His eyes looked frightened to me, . . . especially when we started talking about these subjects, . . . he was so evasive and so frightened."

"Now, have you prepared a list down at Cardinal Glennon of indicators of child sexual abuse?

"Yes."

"On your list . . . you have 28 behavioral indicators of sexual abuse, don't you?"

"That's correct."

". . . All of those also appear in normal children, don't they?"

"Sometimes, yes."

". . . Can you find [frightened] on the behavioral indicator?"

"This list isn't anything that would be exclusive," she explained. It was clear she could add to the list at will and Dr. Monteleone had previously testified that he had based his opinions on her observations.

Charlie interrogated her at length about the use of leading questions in interviewing children about sexual abuse, using her own questions from her videos as examples. "Did someone touch you? Does he hurt you? Does this always happen in your room?" She denied the obvious suggestions inherent in the questioning.

"But if you're asking a child a question and he's telling you no and he says, 'I want to leave now,' and you keep repeating that question, doesn't that suggest to the child that you're looking for an answer of yes?"

"I don't think so."

"Now, did Tim Raymond tell you that Brother Keith put scissors in his bottom?"

"I believe he did, yes."

"And when he said that, did you ask him some details about [it]?"

"I don't think I pursued that, no"

". . . Did you put that in your report that Tim Raymond stated there were scissors put in his bottom?"

"My written description of the videotaped interview is pretty short. No, I didn't put that in." It was apparent LaRock had unquestionable freedom to record arbitrarily whatever she chose.

I was elated when the Court allowed viewing of the video tapes of Tish LaRock interviewing Todd Brady and Tim Raymond, but I wondered if the jury saw what I did. Todd had fifteen different versions of what had allegedly occurred upstairs in the Child Care Center and denied many times that anything had ever happened. Eight times, on the tape, he begged to stop the interview.

On the one video shown in Court, Tim Raymond said he was sick in his body and LaRock rephrased his statement to "bottom" and the stick story evolved. I looked for the fear and nervousness LaRock described in Tim but couldn't see it. Did the jury? On the video, Tim had been told he was making a movie and he was having a ball.

Throughout the video Prosecutor Zimmerman busied himself with jumping up and down, checking the VCR, the jacks, the cords, and he even talked to a deputy once. I couldn't help but wonder if his actions distracted the jurists' minds enough for them to miss the gentle but subtle leading of Ms. LaRock's questions on the video.

By late afternoon the courtroom was hot and stuffy again, and I heard the groan of the antique radiators as they poured out even more heat. It was hard to think clearly and the day was not over yet. The State, however, had just rested it's case. It was 6:45 when Judge Conley dismissed the jury for the evening. For three days now we'd been in the courtroom from 8:30 a.m. until nearly 7 p.m. with only occasional five minute breaks and an hour for lunch. Lynne and I left the courthouse exhausted. We felt deflated, knowing that Charlie had only two days to present my defense if the judge held to his promise that he would not let the trial continue for more than one week.

All I felt like doing when I got home was to collapse in my blue recliner, but the phone rang. It was Laura Rogers calling about the arrival of one of our expert witnesses.

"Brother Keith, Jim and I had no problem finding Dr. Coleman at the airport, however there seems to be a problem here at the St. Charles Holiday Inn. They have no record of his reservation and their rooms are all booked." Laura couldn't miss my sigh over the phone. "To make matters worse," she added, "we have him in a wheel chair. I don't know what's happened other than he recently injured his back and it's causing him extreme pain."

"I'll be there in about five minutes," I promised. Lynne was just serving dinner as I walked out the door. It was a good hour later before I got Dr. Coleman settled into the Ramada Inn and was back home.

"Tomorrow and the after day will decide our future," I told Lynne. As usual, we prayed together before going to sleep and gained some relief. Weary and benumbed from hearing the horrible allegations against me for the past three days, I fell into blessed sleep.

Chapter Eleven

The Verdicts

"The words of Job stood out in my mind:'Though he slay me, I will hope in Him.'"

Thursday, we woke refreshed, anticipating a full day of defense witnesses, including both of our key expert witnesses. Like the other mornings, Lynne, Leanna, and I sat together for a few minutes sipping our morning coffee until almost 8:30 and then left the privacy of our van for the crowded court lobby.

Halfway up the flight of stairs leading to the courtroom was a split landing, and along that landing was a long wooden pew. Since the trial began Monday the Child Care workers had planted themselves there, taking turns encouraging and praying for us all. Continually frustrated for 22 months that they could say nothing on my behalf, they had eagerly waited their turn to testify, fearing only that Zimmerman might trap them into saying something which could be misconstrued and damaging to me and the church.

"Mr. Seibel says you are the type of people he and Charlie want for defense witnesses," I told them when we stopped on the landing. "You're obviously transparent and credible," I said, trying to bolster their confidence. "You'll do just fine."

As we moved on toward the courtroom, several friends who had been subpoenaed to serve as character witnesses stepped up to greet us. We apologized for not having time to visit with them before moving into the court room. The proceeding had just begun when I turned and noticed my brother, Bob, sitting with Lynne and Leanna. It was the only day he had been able to get away from his business and his support was timely.

Bill Seibel handled the direct examinations of the Child Care workers, alternating their testimonies with those of the character witnesses. One by one the workers testified that they had never seen me take a child upstairs or outside the Child Care Center. Their testimonies were enhanced by large charts showing the Child Care work schedule, the hours parents brought and picked up their children, the suggestive and leading questions of interviewers, the dates the children had been interviewed by therapists and police, and the dates on which the children made the accusations against me. These charts alone showed that the offenses of which I was accused could not have happened.

Charles Bridges' wife, Susan, had worked tirelessly in a volunteer capacity for weeks to prepare these charts. My defense attorneys kept the charts before the court the entire week and used them many times as a point of reference in asking questions.

Kathy Haynes had been the only Child Care worker previously interrogated as a possible accomplice. We were totally surprised and puzzled when Zimmerman did not cross-examine her. As she left the stand little Todd's father, obviously agitated, rushed forward to the prosecutor and whispered loudly, "That's the one."

The legal restrictions on a character witness came as a shock to me. I assumed a character witnesses would relate what they knew of a person to be true. However, I found that a character witness is restricted to telling what they have heard others say about you and your reputation in the community. The moment any character witnesses began to refer to their own personal observations of me, Prosecutor Zimmerman objected on the basis of improper response. Still there were times when he didn't get the answer wanted—for example, when he asked Betty Quisinberry, a member of a church I had serving before coming to St. Charles:

"How many times did you talk to people in your community about the defendant's reputation sexually?"

"I don't know that we even discussed that," she replied. "There was no reason to."

When we broke for lunch, Lynne went to look for Dr. Coleman and invite him to eat with us. "He's slender, with a full silver-streaked beard," I told her. She found him sitting stiffly on one of the hallway benches obviously in pain. He purposely declined her invitation to lunch because he preferred not to become personally involved with his clients. Lynne did at least get to thank him for coming to testify.

Meanwhile, I found Dr. ten Bensel. He readily joined us for a salad at Wendy's. In contrast to Dr. Coleman's formal rigidity, Dr. ten Bensel smiled warmly and chatted amiably over lunch, a time that ended too quickly.

After the noon recess Bill Seibel called two more Child Care witnesses, then the attorneys and Judge Conley indulged in a lengthy discussion over admissable evidence. It was after two o'clock before Charlie called Dr. Coleman to the stand.

He hardly looked like the man we saw earlier sitting stiffly in his solitary chair. He stood erect and walked smoothly, evidencing not a trace of pain, and appearing as a solid wall of strength. In answer to Charlie's questions, he familiarized us with his schooling, his medical degree from the University of Chicago, his pediatric internship from Children's Medical Center in Seattle, and four years in general and child psychiatry at the University of Colorado Medical Center in Denver from 1965-69.

Since the early seventies his main interests, he said, had centered in adult and child clinical practice and psychiatry as related to law.

Charlie continued. "[Have you] written any articles or books that have been published?"

"I have one book. It's called *The Reign of Error*, [and] . . . at last count 32 articles which deal with a variety of these topics."

"[You have] published in national recognized psychiatric journals?

"Yes."

". . . Explain to the jury . . . the experience you've had in regards to sexual abuse allegations by children."

". . . I have reviewed somewhere between 150-200 cases. . . . I've had a chance to listen to somewhere between 500-600 hours of . . . taped interviews. . . . I have testified that the techniques of psychiatry and psychology even in the best of hands do not allow us to get inside somebody's head with any reliability to determine whether they knew right from wrong."

"In your studies regarding false allegations [of sexual abuse of children] are they a rare occurrence across the country or what's the situation?"

"No, they're not rare."

"Now, in the cases that you have studied, is it a situation

where the child normally knows what they are claiming is false, they're deliberately lying. . .?

". . . The issue," Dr. Coleman explained, "is whether or not the child has their own memory, . . . or whether or not because of repeated questioning in interviewing in an improper way, the child has basically come to conjecture and speculate and imagine, and possibilities, which if repeated often enough, the child actually comes to believe in. And then the child is speaking just as sincerely as if they had experienced it."

". . . Has your experience been in your studies that that's normally something intentionally done by the interviewer . . . ?"

"Well, I can't read minds anymore than anybody else. . . . My own feeling is it's training [in] improper techniques and improper style which . . . interviewers are in good conscience carrying out. . . . A lot of pressure gets put on people in the investigative agencies to essentially adapt what they would call a supportive attitude, which means believe that it did happen because then you become one of the people that is on the good side of protecting children. . . . That leads to a very aggressive style of interviewing a child in the name of helping them . . . which has the danger of causing a non-molested child to talk about it because they pick up the attitude that you have."

Charlie posed another question. "What are some of the contaminating factors that you have identified through your studies . . . in regards to suggestive or leading questions of children?"

"Well, the most important thing of all is the attitude of the interviewer. And next will come the behavior of the interviewer. But the behavior is going to be a reflection of the attitude. . . . Interviewers appear to behave in such a way which could only be explained that they have a belief that something happened from the virtual beginning of the interviews."

Dr. Coleman continued to explain how questions that contain elements of the answer, teach the child what the interviewer thinks. "Another problem is . . . how the interviewer responds to the question. Let's say . . . the child said 'no'. . . . The interviewer says, . . . 'Are you sure? Would that be hard to talk about?, Other kids have told us. . . .' The child can pick up the idea that the interviewer would rather hear that it happened than that it didn't happen."

In response to questions about the use of anatomically correct dolls and role-playing with instructions to show or pretend, Dr. Coleman replied, "The very activity itself . . . —that's what kids do when they tell stories and when they imagine things and that's the worst possible way to help a child understand that we only want to know what you can remember from your actual memory and nothing but that."

"Now," Charlie said, "I'd like to go to the group interview and ask you your comments as to that."

". . . A group interview is the worst, most contaminating thing . . . . I can't think of a better way of starting a rumor mill than to put a bunch of people together and interview them on the same subject where you want to get their independent memory."

Charlie asked about the significant behaviors identifying sexually abused children. Dr. Coleman replied, "There is no way that you can take regressive behavior or any other behavior pattern and use it to help decide whether a child has been abused . . . , there's too many other things that could cause the same behaviors. It's non-specific."

During cross-exam, Zimmerman tried to cast a shadow on Coleman's credentials because some of his articles had been printed in *Hustler* and *Chick* magazines. Asked to describe the magazines, Coleman said the[y] . . . covered a wide range of social issues. "They are pornographic as far as the pictures," which he described as tasteless.

At 5:30 Dr. Coleman finally stepped down from the witness stand. Judge Conley announced a ten minute recess after which Dr. ten Bensel was called to the stand as our second expert witness. In addition to his medical degree from Harvard Medical School, Dr. ten Bensel said he had completed a pediatric residency and a master's degree in public health, and during 19 years as a practicing pediatrician had examined over 50,000 patients.

Besides over 50 articles in pediatrics and public health, he had written a book chapter on adolescent maltreatment, written and produced two television programs, and participated in developing training manuals for the National College of Juvenile and Family Court Judges. Impressive credentials.

"Dr. ten Bensel, are you involved on a national committee with the U.S. Surgeon General?" Charlie asked.

"Last year, . . . Surgeon General Koop, along with Attorney

General Meese put together a panic committee of eight people to develop what was called a law health initiative on child sexual abuse because of the need to bring physicians together with law enforcement around having a standardized protocol for the assessments of child sexual abuse in this country."

"You agree that you base your expertise on your . . . experience?"

"Expertise is based upon training and upon experience and upon a code of ethics. Those are the three criteria to be an expert."

"Before we get into questions . . . , could you draw for the jury just briefly a description of a child's anus . . . ?"

"I guess what I'll do is modify this particular diagram," Dr. ten Bensel said as he stepped to a white board and skillfully drew a detailed sagittal section, the pubic bone in front and coccyx in back. He continued to talk and draw, naming specific body parts, rectum, anus, coccyx, while giving a description and function of each as he proceeded.

". . . If I have my finger in the [child's] rectum and my thumb on the outside, that—that's only about a very short distance. . . , less than a quarter of an inch until you feel the bone. . . ."

Dr. ten Bensel completed his diagram and returned to the witness stand. Charlie resumed his direct exam.

"What is the recommended procedure in the standards in the medical profession as to documenting findings in child sexual abuse cases?"

"Well, clearly you have to have the history. You have to have the physical exam and appropriate laboratory work and then do a differential diagnosis." Dr. ten Bensel's genuinely warm personality radiated through his constant smile.

". . . Documentation is critical for the basis of making reports. . . . If there were positive findings, you would diagram those. . . . The standard practice is to take photographs of all abnormalities, particularly in the area of child abuse and neglect because those have to be reviewed by police. . . , [and] social service . . . , if it becomes a legal matter."

"Would it be standard procedure," Charlie asked, "for a doctor not to photograph evidence of child sexual abuse if he would find a scar on the anus or any other evidence?"

". . . Anyone who works with the legal system knows a

photographic documentation is really essential to most legal cases. . . . I've never seen an exception to them being documented. They are always documented by photography."

"Is this the first case that you have been involved in where it has not been documented by photography?"

"I have never—right, this is the first case."

"What is the significance of the finding in [Dr. Monteleone's] report of where he indicates [a] small scar on the anus?"

". . . [The] standard practice is that one would measure that in millimeters or in inches."

"Have you ever in your experience," Charlie wanted to know, "encountered a situation where not only does a doctor not photograph but he does not describe the shape, the length, or the location of the scar?"

"I have never seen a record that has lack of definition as the statement here."

"If a stick enters . . . as far as three to four inches into the rectum and still only leave[s] a centimeter[-] or a millimeter[-long] scar, is that possible?"

"In my experience, that's not possible. . . . It's right up against the bone. . . . If I had that history, I would have sought out consultation."

"What type of damage would you expect to find in a child that has a history of a stick [3/4" - 1" in diameter] entering into the rectum?"

"You can have perforating injuries. . . . It would be terrible damage. It would be just like jamming a stick into a little girl's vagina at the same age. That tissue is very thin and very delicate. There would be blood, a tremendous history of pain, . . . immediate pain."

It was past 6:30 and I was concerned that Doctor ten Benzel might miss his flight to Minneapolis, due to leave in one hour, when Prosecutor Zimmerman assigned Charles Lampin, a new prosecuting assistant fresh from law school, to cross-examine Dr. ten Bensel. I was embarrassed for Dr. ten Bensel when Lampin referred to the doctor's hands-on experience with 50,000 cases as ancient history and appalled when Lampin asked if Dr. Monteleone wasn't more qualified to give an opinion.

Dr. ten Bensel kept his gracious smile and calmly disagreed, then proceeded to name several more of his positions and accomplishments not mentioned before.

Lampin was still not satisfied. "Now, Doctor, you agree that it is of utmost importance to know what the size of the object was in determining the amount of injury. Correct?" .... If it's small, then the injury may be minimal, if not non-existent. Correct?"

"Well, quite the contrary. I mean, an ice pick, if you sit on an ice pick versus a baseball bat, an ice pick will do more harm to you than a baseball bat because it's big and blunt." Almost the entire court room broke up in laughter, providing a kind of comic relief that helped ease the tension.

Harold Hendrick had his van at the door when Dr. ten Bensel, the last witness for the day, left the courtroom at 7:10. As we rushed him to the waiting van I thanked him and added, "If you hit all green lights, you just might make it."

The expressions of the jurists still gave no clues to their thoughts but I went home feeling almost excited. When I turned the TV channel to "L.A. Law," Lynne and Leanna reacted in unison, "Haven't you had enough courtroom drama for one day?"

Friday morning I woke to a strange mixture of incongruous feelings. Fear and faith fought when I contemplated what the day might bring. Would my ordeal be over? Would the trial continue into the next week? Or would testimony be completed in time for a verdict to be reached today? And would the decision force me to make the appeal which Charlie and I had discussed before the trial began?

Lynne and I discussed my wearing a bullet proof vest on this last day. Remembering the open hostility at the arraignment made the idea seem justifiable. Would not wearing one be an exercise in faith or foolishness? We bounced the idea around awhile before tossing it out.

All week we'd been the first to arrive at the courthouse, but Friday morning, the Gaylords and Bradys, along with their friends, were already in the lobby, standing next to the locked courtroom doors, dressed fit for a wedding and laughing merrily, when we walked up.

"They seem to be expecting great things today," Leanna observed. As soon as a bailiff unlocked the courtroom doors they rushed en masse and fanned out across all the front pews, scattering their purses and coats around them. It seemed a petty thing for adults to do. Lynne was determined not to show irritation as she walked to the side section and sat in the first open pew which happened to be directly behind the Walkers. She wanted to be emotionally ready when Bill Seibel called her as a witness.

She opened her purse and scanned the dozens of verses she had written on yellow Post-it Notes. Her eyes rested on some sentences from Psalms 18, "He delivered me from my strong enemy. . . . He makes my feet like hinds' feet, and sets me upon high places. . . . My feet have not slipped."

Lea Haney, my "Attack" secretary, was scheduled as the next witness. She waited alone on the long pew on the stairway landing just below the courtroom when a commotion attracted her attention. Out of sight from where she sat she heard a man ask, "What trial's going on here?"

"Oh, that Barnhart case," someone answered.

"They oughta hang him," a second person chimed in.

"I'll get a rope," another volunteered just as the bailiff came to the door and called Lea's name. She was angry and frightened as she entered the courtroom to testify.

Bill asked her only a few general questions, then turned her over to Zimmerman for an expected grilling on cross-exam. To her relief, the prosecutor's questioning was brief and benign.

Lynne followed Lea to the stand. Bill's disarming manner put her at ease as he led her through a short direct exam. Bill looked at Zimmerman.

To almost everybody's surprise Zimmerman said, "Nothing your honor."

The judge looked at Bill Seibel. "Call your next witness."

Bill was ready, but was I? "Call Reverend Keith Barnhart to the stand."

I stood and drew a deep breath. Prompted by habit, I buttoned my suit jacket as I walked across the front of the courtroom. My hands were cold. My heart beat frantically when I stepped up into the witness stand, and turned to look briefly into the staring eyes of my accusers. After I was sworn in, Bill stepped directly into my view, smiled reassuringly, and began my direct exam.

He obligingly asked about my past and present employment, education, honors and awards, and my wife and children—all routine questions. Then he focused attention on the Child Care Center at the church. He asked about the history of the Center, my relationship to it, my work schedule, my attendance at denominational meetings, etc. etc.

Zimmerman objected to this line of questioning. "Your Honor, . . . I don't think it's relevant to the case. And I think it's improper bolstering of this witness.

Judge Conley overruled the prosecutor's objection.

Bill then questioned me in detail about my relationship to the children who had made the allegations. He struck no new ground. I merely repeated information which I had given to the police and my attorneys.

Bill neared the conclusion of his examination of me, the defendant.

"And you're telling this jury here today that you never molested either [Chad Walker or Todd Brady], or any other child at the Daycare Center; is that correct?

"I have never molested or abused any child. I have never done that."

"Anywhere; is that correct?

"Anywhere."

"And you're swearing to that under oath, is that the truth?"

"So help me, God, yes."

"No further questions."

Judge Conley looked at the prosecutor. "Cross."

Zimmerman stood and walked towards me. "Thank you, Your Honor."

After a few routine questions, Zimmerman got down to business. "When did you find out about all this stuff going on?"

"[I] first became aware of some accusations, December 10th."

". . . Over three months between the time you found out about this and when you were arrested; isn't that right?"

"Three or four months."

"And your first act, Mr. Barnhart, was not to show up at the Christmas program on December 12th, isn't that correct?"

"That was because I was at the police station, sir." Zimmerman gave no sign of even hearing my answer.

"You never appeared, did you?" He wouldn't let me answer, he just kept interrupting.

"It's true, isn't it that you never for three months, three solid months, you never tried to contact anyone in an effort to clear up what you felt was just a terrible mistake?"

"After [I was] questioned by the police, . . . the attorney advised me not to discuss it with the parties involved." Again

Zimmerman gave no acknowledgement of my answer.

"You're a minister, aren't you?"

"Yes, I am."

"And isn't it true that when these accusations came out you acted like a defendant and not like a minister?"

"I."

"I'll object." I felt relief when Bill Seibel interrupted. "That's argumentative." There was further discussion then Zimmerman tried another angle.

"You love kids, don't you?"

"I like kids. I like adults. I like young people." I felt like I was playing a deadly version of 'cat and mouse.' Thinking and speaking fast had never been my forte, so I measured each word carefully. I wondered what the jury would think if I blushed. Would they misconstrue what was as normal for me as breathing?"

"O.K., and you're a minister and by doing that your job is to help people, especially through difficult times, wouldn't that be true?"

"I believe so."

"O.K. Yet you know that Todd Brady and Tim Raymond . . . . were having a tremendous problem and that you apparently were the cause of that problem and you never tried to help?"

"But I was not the cause of the problem. . . ," I challenged.

"Isn't it true that you just never lifted a single Christian finger to try to help anyone in this case as a minister?" I knew Zimmerman had no facts and no proof and his gouging questions were a desperate attempt to discredit me. Logic, however, had little immediate effect on the emotional hurricane churning inside me. I felt the familiar tingle of blood creeping slowly up my neck and spreading over my face.

"And you're staking your liberty on convincing everyone here that these children were just suggested and manipulated into these answers and you didn't do a thing? Is that true?"

"I have never touched those boys or any other children, sir, alone or molested any other or sexually abused them. . . . I know that I've been falsely accused. I've never done this." Zimmerman's cross examination was brutal. My knees felt weak when I stepped down from the stand.

It was mid-afternoon when Judge Conley finished his instructions to the jury. Then he directed his attention to Mr.

Zimmerman and soberly intoned, "Argument for the state."

The Court allowed 20 minutes to each for closing arguments, however the State's time was divided into two 10-minute periods, with the defending attorney's 20-minute statement in between.

"Thank you, Your Honor," Zimmerman acknowledged. He stepped briskly to the jury bar. With a dramatic flourish, he began his closing arguments. "Ladies and Gentlemen, it has been a long week and you can sort of smell it in the air. . . . I think the greatest fear in this case is that when you put those two small boys on the stand . . . the jury will end up forgetting about them."

He shifted his focus to the Child Care workers. With a theatrical swing of his arms, he declared, "I'm here to tell you that the State is not saying that those Day Care Center workers are lying, . . . but . . . everyone automatically believed in the innocence of the defendant."

Zimmerman stood on his toes when he took a verbal swing at Dr. Coleman and me. "Now I'm not going to get all involved with the particular magazines that he's published in, but I think it gives you an idea of the character of the man. And it gives you an idea of the kind of man who would hire him."

Zimmerman's first time period for his closing argument ran out. Charlie walked calmly to the jury box and laid his notes on the railing. With his deep steady voice he took full command.

". . . In our country we have a system of justice where the prosecutor has to prove beyond a reasonable doubt that the defendant is guilty. If he doesn't do that, then the defendant is protected by the presumption of innocence. . . . It's clear in this case that it is the State that has been using every tactic it can to keep the truth from you, they don't want you to hear how this case developed. They don't want you to hear what went on in this case. This is just the opposite of what normally occurs."

Charlie's voice was strong as he skillfully elaborated on points he felt the jury should consider. "Tish LaRock . . . testified under oath that she's got a bachelor's degree, . . . If she's going to lie about something like that. . . ."

"Dr. Monteleone said, '. . . This is consistent with sexual abuse and that's my opinion. But don't go get a second opinion.' . . . I tell you if a [professional] came to me . . . and told me, 'Here's my diagnosis, but don't get a second opinion,' that would be the first thing I [would do]. That's the first clue that you have someone who's incompetent."

Charlie's voice was full and controlled as he methodically reviewed several inconsistencies in the children's statements as well as those of the State's professionals. Relentlessly, he used facts, not theatrics, to drive his point home. "You hear Dr. Monteleone when cross-examined on articles that he said are authoritative. Books from his very library. American Medical Association books. Nothing that he found is supported in any of those books. . . . "

"He tells you that the stick that went into a child's rectum and caused the same damage that an oversized stool can cause. And he must think we are idiots."

Charlie was so totally absorbed in his convictions and his statements about Dr. Monteleone about the stick and the scissors incident that he surprised us all by saying, ". . . He said that about the scissors stuck up here? Would that cause any damage? No. No. That wouldn't cause any. We ought to have someone stick scissors in his." Loud laughter swept across the courtroom.

Judge Conley beat his gavel for order. "Ladies and Gentlemen, let me ask you please to refrain from your expressions."

Zimmerman came back for his second and final 10-minute closing. In reference to my attorney, Charlie Bridges, the prosecutor said, "He's a little man who has decided that his case has all blown up. . . . Before I got on top of this case, I was your average everyday prosecutor . . . ; now I've become sort of a local expert on this."

Zimmerman turned to Dr. Coleman. "[He] runs around the country doing nothing but this. And getting paid big bucks to do it. Fifteen hundred bucks a day. I'll tell you what, I know more, based upon what I've done, than this guy [Dr. Coleman] does about suggestible and interview technique."

He started again and was interrupted by the bailiff. "Counselor, time."

"Well, I guess I won't—Ladies and Gentlemen, I want to thank you for your attention. Like I said, don't trust me, trust them." He obviously meant my accusers.

Judge Conley gave the jury their instructions and dismissed them to deliberate. The formality of the courtroom relaxed as people began gathering in knots. I saw clusters of our friends talking softly, some with heads bowed in prayer.

Families and friends of my accusers picked up with their laughter of the morning. They seemed relaxed, confident, at ease.

I saw Andy talk with the bailiffs then go to Bob Hull, one of our church officers present. "There's some threats rumored around, Bob." It was good I didn't hear him. Unknown to me at the time, Bob agreed to watch from the front of the room and Andy the back.

About an hour and fifty minutes later I saw the jury room door crack open. As one bailiff headed for the Judge's chambers, another bailiff came to me. "We'd like you to sit here," he instructed. I moved and saw three bailiffs close in behind me.

I turned to see Lynne and Leanna both tense when they saw the Judge step out.

We were all aware of the importance of the moment, and waited silently on an emotional edge too fragile for words.

A smothering silence settled over the room as Judge Conley took his seat. "Ladies and Gentlemen, . . . the court is going to make two statements. . . . Number one, anybody who is in the courtroom when the jury comes in is going to remain . . . until the jury has left the St. Charles County Courthouse. . . . "

"Number two, I know the emotions are extremely high in this case. Regardless of what the verdicts may be, . . . I hope [you] will conduct yourself appropriately, that there will not be any vocal displays. . . . I'm going to enforce that requirement and if I have difficulty then I'm going to have the sheriff's department remove you from the courtroom. So please conduct yourself appropriately.

"Bring the jury in."

The brief moments it took for the jurists to take their seats felt like an endless eternity. The words of Job stood out in my mind. "Though He slay me, I will hope in Him."

"Mr. Foreman," Judge Conley instructed, "will you deliver the verdict to the bailiff, please, together with the instructions."

I thought the judge was preparing to read the verdict. Instead he thanked the jury and instructed them on how to leave the courtroom. Then he repeated the two lengthy statements he had made just before calling in the jury.

How much longer can he draw this out? I wondered. My clammy fingers shook when I pushed back the top of my shirt cuff to look at my watch. How long, O Lord, how long? I was sure Judge Conley must be done talking, but he wasn't.

The judge spoke about a post-trial let-down "that's going to set in for each one of you . . . about 12 hours down the road. . . ."

Then he commended the attorneys for conducting themselves "in a very professional manner in a case that is highly charged with emotions . . . " He expressed appreciation to the jury again. Finally, he said in a dry voice with no trace of a smile, "Now I'm going to read the verdicts and then you will be at liberty to leave the courtroom."

"As to Count One, . . . not guilty." I stopped breathing. "As to Count Two, . . . not guilty." I drew the deepest breath I'd drawn in 22 long months. Tears of joy welled up in my eyes and deep, deep relief surged through my tired, tense mind.

I looked around and saw teary smiles on the faces of Lynne, Leanna, and our devoted friends. I saw the distraught parents gasping in shock. I couldn't help but hurt for these shattered families, victims behind an invisible wall built by trusted but misguided professionals.

Two days later I sat beside Lynne in church and watched Leanna on the platform. With large, free sweeping gestures she "signed" in the beautiful langauge of the deaf the lyrics to a majestic rendition of the song, "Lord of All."

"Lord of All," she signed, and I realized anew the underlying belief that had seen us through these almost two years. Lynne's hand was nestled in mine as the truth of the eloquently signed words filled the air with the expressions of our hearts. God was truly Lord of all. He had lifted us from the depths of despair that threatened to tear our faith apart. I knew that in future days He would enable me to lift my head high among these people I loved. At last, after so many assumptions that I was guilty, I had been declared innocent. I was free.

Afterword

Eighteen months have passed since my acquittal. Just two weeks ago we stood beside the grave of Lynne's dear father. This week, as we were checking final manuscript copy, I assisted my mother in placing Dad in a care center. Such events make us more keenly aware of bonds to our families and their sacrifice for us during these past years.

Lynne and I are thankful for the resiliency of our own children. Both Emily, now 15, and Matthew, 13, seem well adjusted both at home and school. We trust that they have witnessed through our lives that God can be trusted.

I continue as pastor of Cave Springs Baptist Church. Our church family and area pastors remain supportive. However, the stigma of my ordeal has changed my ministry. I maintain a distance from church programs involving children and I never allow myself to be alone in a room with a child, other than my own. I'm also aware that in the future I can never consider a church that operates a child care facility. In the minds of some people there will always remain a shadow of doubt about my innocence.

An occasional harassing phone call keeps that awareness alive. Last spring, a boy called my office. "Tell Brother Keith," he said to my secretary, Lea, "that next time I see him I'm going to slap him in the face." It's frightening to think I could answer the phone and find myself speaking to one of the little boys, and then be accused of trying to make contact with them .

With only one exception, the workers who once served in the permanently closed Cave Springs Baptist Child Care Center avoid contact with small children because they are afraid to express the love they feel. These dedicated women still struggle with the loss of what for most of them had become their life's work. They dare not risk the chance of their names ever being associated with accusations of child abuse. Just how big is that risk? A study by VOCAL in Missouri found one of every 37 households in our state touched by false accusations.

Am I and these women overreacting? Not according to a recent statement from findings filed by an area circuit judge, the Honorable John D. Chancellor, relating to a pending child abuse case. Said the judge: "They [alleged child abusers] are the most difficult to defend because the very mention of the charge tends to cast a cloak of guilt over the accused, which makes a fair trial somewhat of an elusive proposition."[15]

I am frequently asked, "Why don't you sue the 'professionals' for their handling of your case?" Even if I wished to do so, Missouri law allows no legal recourse against any agent of the state. As I stated in the book, all mandated reporters, including therapists, health professionals, and law enforcement personnel, have complete immunity, even if they have misrepresented their findings.

The chance of a fair trial for the increasing number of persons so accused is becoming even more remote. This is especially true in Missouri. According to Charlie Bridges, my chief defense attorney, the St. Charles Police have stopped videotaping interviews of children. They have learned from my case that if the jury sees the videos, the use of suggestive and leading questions becomes undeniable. Without videotaped interviews, jurors are more likely to believe the police who testify under oath that their questions of young children are not leading and suggestive.

As soon as a verdict in the McMartin Trial was rendered in California, Channel Four of St. Louis called me for an interview. This gave me the opportunity to announce that my book was soon to be released. Before the night was over, I got a phone call from one of the parents making the charges against me. "Why?" she asked sarcastically. "It's over. Why? What's your point?"

My point is that it isn't over. Just a few days ago our answering machine recorded a male voice that threatened, "Brother Keith, when was the last time you molested little children? Your church is gonna be blown up with you and your family and all the congregation. Have a nice day."

No, it isn't all over. Not for myself and not for thousands of others who have been falsely accused, and not for the many little children who have been abused by the professionals in their zealous effort to help prosecutors obtain a conviction.

I'm telling my story to encourage and help victims who

don't have the love and support I did. I'm writing so others can see for themselves how, in Dr. ten Bensel's words, "the system . . . has gone awry," and how our trusted, but misguided professionals have become like gods, beyond scrutiny and accountable to no one.

Beyond all this, this book is presented with a prayer that those caught up in the child abuse nightmare may find, as Lynne and I did, healing and strength from the Lord of all.

Sources

Following are sources for material cited in the text as helpful in understanding my case and in preparing my defense. The numbers correspond to inscriptions in the book.

1. Lee Coleman, M.D.: "Has a Child Been Molested?" *Opinion*, July, 1986, p. 15.

2 William D. Slicker, Attorney at Law: "Child Sex Abuse: The Innocent Accused," *Case and Comment*, November-December, 1986, p. 12.

3. Mary Pride: *The Child Abuse Industry*. Crossway Books, 1986, p. ix.

4. Sidney L. Williams, Attorney at Law: "When a Child Points the Finger," *St. Louis Post-Dispatch*, April 19, 1987.

5. Pride, op. cit., p. 49.

6. Hollida Wakefield and Ralph Underwager, M.D.: *"Accusations of Child Sexual Abuse,"* Charles C. Thomas Publisher, 1988.

7. Robert W. Peterson: "Child Abuse Suspects Lose Right to Confront Accuser," *San Jose (California) Mercury News*, May 5, 1987, p. 7B.

8. Robert L. Emans: "Abuse in the name of Protecting Children," *Phi Delta Kappan*, June, 1987, p. 741.

9. Wm. F. McIver, Ph.D., Letter, December 15, 1986.

10. Wakefield & Underwager, op. cit.,

11. Emans, op. cit. 1987.

12. Coleman, op. cit.

13. James Monteleone, M.D.: Transcript of General Comments at Ninth Missouri Child Abuse and Neglect Conference, May 4, 1988.

14. Charles E. Bridges: *Distinguishing Between True and False Allegations of Child Sexual Abuse [and] Allegations of Child Sexual Abuse in Divorce Cases: Response to Criminal Charges, Bridges, Nichols, and Seibel*, St. Charles, MO.

15. The Honorable John D. Chancellor, Circuit Court, St. Louis, MO., *Findings of Fact, Conclusions of Law, Judgement, and Decrees*, 1989.

All Bible quotations are from the New American Standard Bible.

Additional Recommended Reading

NASVO NEWS (National Association of State Vocal Oragnizations), 9520 Flintridge Way, Orangvale, CA. 95662 or 1769 66th St. N., St. Petersburg, FL. 33710

Lee Coleman, M.D.: "Medical Examination for Sexual Abuse: Have We Been Misled? *Issues in Child Abuse Accusations,* 1989, Vol. 1, p. 1.

Lawrence Spiegel: *"A Question of Innocence,"* Unicorn Publishing House, Morris Plains, NJ, 1986.

Domeena C. Renshaw, M.D.: "When Sex Abuse is Falsely Charged," *The Champion,* January/February, 1986, p. 8.

Debbie Nathan Voice, "The Making of a Modern Witch Trial," *Voice,* September 29, 1987.

Tom Charlier and Shirley Downing: "Justice Abused, a 1980's Witch Hunt," *The Commercial Appeal,* Memphis, TN., Parts 1-6, January, 1988.

William F. McIver, Ph.D.: "The Cases for a Therapeutic Interview in Situations of Alleged Sexual Molestation," *The Champion,* January/February, 1986, p. 11.

Paul and Shirley Eberle: *Policies of Child Abuse* Lyle Stuart Inc., Secaucus, New Jersey, 1986.

Please send me . . . .

Guilty Until Proven Innocent by Keith Barnhart with Lila Shelburne. Dramatic true story of the prosecution of an innocent pastor charged with sexual child abuse. A must book for all who work with children.

_____ Copies at $9.95 = _____

90 Days for Life by Fred Kerr. A spiritual journal by a minister in jail for protesting abortion.

_____ Copies at $7.95 = _____

Where Is God When a Child Suffers? by Penny Giesbrecht. How a Christian family copes with their child's pain in the light of God's love.

_____ Copies at $8.95 = _____

12 plus me by Pat. Likes. A warm, true family story of growing up on a farm in the Mississippi River bootoms inthe late 30's and early 50's.

_____ Copies at $7.95 = _____

The Greatest Book Ever Written by Dr. Rochunga Pudaite with James C. Hefley, Ph.D. Praised by evangelical leaders as an outstanding apologetic on the Bible.

_____ Copies at $9.95 = _____

COMING SOON FROM HANNIBAL BOOKS

*We Can Change America . . . and Here's How"*by Darylann Whitemarsh. How to make things happen in the public arena. Especially helpful for pro-lifers to use in coming battles to save the unborn.

_____ Copies at $9.95 = _____

Please add $2.00 postage and handling for first book, plus .50 for each additional book.

Shipping & Handling _____

MO residents add sales tax _____

TOTAL ENCLOSED (Check or money order)_____

Name _____

Address _____

City_____State____ Zip _____Phone_____

MAIL TO HANNIBAL BOOKS,921 Center, Hannibal, MO 63401.
Satisfaction guaranteed. Call 314-221-2462 for quantity prices.

Please send me . . . .

Guilty Until Proven Innocent by Keith Barnhart with Lila Shelburne. Dramatic true story of the prosecution of an innocent pastor charged with sexual child abuse. A must book for all who work with children.

_____ Copies at $9.95 = _____

90 Days for Life by Fred Kerr. A spiritual journal by a minister in jail for protesting abortion.

_____ Copies at $7.95 = _____

Where Is God When a Child Suffers? by Penny Giesbrecht. How a Christian family copes with their child's pain in the light of God's love.

_____ Copies at $8.95 = _____

12 plus me by Pat. Likes. A warm, true family story of growing up on a farm in the Mississippi River bootoms inthe late 30's and early 50's.

_____ Copies at $7.95 = _____

The Greatest Book Ever Written by Dr. Rochunga Pudaite with James C. Hefley, Ph.D. Praised by evangelical leaders as an outstanding apologetic on the Bible.

_____ Copies at $9.95 = _____

COMING SOON FROM HANNIBAL BOOKS

We Can Change America . . . and Here's How" by Darylann Whitemarsh. How to make things happen in the public arena. Especially helpful for pro-lifers to use in coming battles to save the unborn.

_____ Copies at $9.95 = _____

Please add $2.00 postage and handling for first book, plus .50 for each additional book.

Shipping & Handling _____

MO residents add sales tax _____

TOTAL ENCLOSED (Check or money order)_____

Name _____

Address _____

City_____State____ Zip _____Phone_____

MAIL TO HANNIBAL BOOKS,921 Center, Hannibal, MO 63401. Satisfaction guaranteed. Call 314-221-2462 for quantity prices.

Please send me . . . .

Guilty Until Proven Innocent by Keith Barnhart with Lila Shelburne. Dramatic true story of the prosecution of an innocent pastor charged with sexual child abuse. A must book for all who work with children.

_____ Copies at $9.95 = _____

90 Days for Life by Fred Kerr. A spiritual journal by a minister in jail for protesting abortion.

_____ Copies at $7.95 = _____

Where Is God When a Child Suffers? by Penny Giesbrecht. How a Christian family copes with their child's pain in the light of God's love.

_____ Copies at $8.95 = _____

12 plus me by Pat. Likes. A warm, true family story of growing up on a farm in the Mississippi River bootoms inthe late 30's and early 50's.

_____ Copies at $7.95 = _____

The Greatest Book Ever Written by Dr. Rochunga Pudaite with James C. Hefley, Ph.D. Praised by evangelical leaders as an outstanding apologetic on the Bible.

_____ Copies at $9.95 = _____

COMING SOON FROM HANNIBAL BOOKS

We Can Change America . . . and Here's How" by Darylann Whitemarsh. How to make things happen in the public arena. Especially helpful for pro-lifers to use in coming battles to save the unborn.

_____ Copies at $9.95 = _____

Please add $2.00 postage and handling for first book, plus .50 for each additional book.

Shipping & Handling _____

MO residents add sales tax _____

TOTAL ENCLOSED (Check or money order) _____

Name _____

Address _____

City _____ State ____ Zip _____ Phone_____

MAIL TO HANNIBAL BOOKS, 921 Center, Hannibal, MO 63401. Satisfaction guaranteed. Call 314-221-2462 for quantity prices.